"This marvelously crafted and deeply moving love letter to the tender and beautiful connections between spirit and gender is a true gift to the world. Ariana Serpentine takes the reader on an exploration of gender, identity, and expression within the context of embodied, lived spiritual practice. I cannot recommend this book enough. Whether you are someone who identifies as transgender, are exploring your identity, or simply someone wishing to learn more about gender, this is a must read. Filled with eye-opening exercises and an overflowing cauldron of knowledge, this is a book that I will treasure for many moons to come."

—Mhara Starling, author of *Welsh Witchcraft*

SACRED GENDER

About the Author

Ariana Serpentine is a multi-traditional witch, polytheist, and animist. She is transgender and queer and has worked in political trans activism, raising awareness for the needs of her community within Pagan and other circles.

Ariana Serpentine

SACRED GENDER

CREATE
TRANS & NONBINARY
SPIRITUAL
CONNECTIONS

Llewellyn Publications • Woodbury, Minnesota

FIRST EDITION
First Printing, 2022

Book design by Samantha Peterson
Cover design by Shira Atakpu

Llewellyn Publications is a registered trademark of Llewellyn Worldwide Ltd.

Library of Congress Cataloging-in-Publication Data (Pending)
ISBN: 978-0-7387-7134-2

Llewellyn Worldwide Ltd. does not participate in, endorse, or have any authority or responsibility concerning private business transactions between our authors and the public.
  All mail addressed to the author is forwarded but the publisher cannot, unless specifically instructed by the author, give out an address or phone number.
  Any internet references contained in this work are current at publication time, but the publisher cannot guarantee that a specific location will continue to be maintained. Please refer to the publisher's website for links to authors' websites and other sources.

Llewellyn Publications
A Division of Llewellyn Worldwide Ltd.
2143 Wooddale Drive
Woodbury, MN 55125-2989
www.llewellyn.com

Printed in the United States of America

For the trans Ancestors, the ones who have gone before me: I hope that my work has honored you.

For the trans descendants, the ones who will come after me: I hope that my work has made the world better for you.

For every trans person: May you find the sacred within and see yourself among the stars.

CONTENTS

EXERCISE LIST

ACKNOWLEDGMENTS

Thanks to River Devora, Morgan Daimler, Chelydoreus, Martiana, and everyone else who helped me find sources.

Thanks to Maur for the Smile Test that has served me so well over the years.

Thanks to Misha Magdalene for being an inspiration, guide, and cheerleader.

Thanks again to River for supporting me through the process and believing in me.

Thanks to Nick Walker Hirsch, Misha, River, and all of my test readers for your feedback and patience.

Thanks to Rianorix and the Toys in Creation for helping to plant the seed that grew into this tree.

Thanks to Dionysos, Ariadne, Hermes, the Great Mother Kybele, and all of the gods, spirits, and Ancestors who contributed to this work.

FOREWORD

In the beginning there was nothing. No, that isn't true, the universe has never been truly empty. But what is a beginning? Where do we begin to tell our stories? In our beginning, there were chains of increasingly complex molecules, joining and breaking and reforming into new shapes, creating new possibilities. Those possibilities became cells; those cells formed colonies; those colonies took on complex identities, bathed in the first waters, warmed by the same sun that shines overhead as I write this. In the beginning, there were neither "men" nor "women" because those are modern human concepts deeply shaped by whatever our individual and collective cultural contexts are currently. And even those cultural contexts keep shifting and changing, chains of molecular possibilities forming and breaking and reforming into new things.

My own favorite story of beginnings is that, in the beginning, the most relevant beginning, there was a fire. And folks contained that fire, kept it fed and properly banked, and gathered around it to keep safe and warm, to tell stories and cook food and keep the dark at bay. And from that fire, webs formed, connecting individuals into a stable network of care and shared resources. In the beginning was the creation of the web of interdependence, the web of creation, the web of life. Each strand separable, unique, bringing its own beauty and strength to contribute to the complexity and stability of the weaving. There, see? Room for everyone in a story like that, isn't there? There are many beginnings. That one is my personal favorite.

I vaguely remember my own beginnings in terms of trying to make sense of my gender. I didn't like it; I didn't understand it. Gender seemed to be a set of frightening and arbitrary rules that I kept discovering by cutting myself on their sharp and hidden edges. Gender was one more set of nonintuitive, invisible structures that I was supposed to magically know were there, one more thing for me to fail at. Parts of me seemed to put me firmly in one of the two available boxes in the eyes of the folks who decided these things. Parts of me didn't properly fit the boxes, and I was shamed and belittled for not fitting boxes I hadn't actually chosen due to criteria and factors beyond my control. My body, not quite right. My interests and passions, the things I loved, not right. The religion I was raised in said G-d made us that way, that these were things inherent to our souls, that "boys" and "girls" got different rules and different options. This was not a game I was ever going to succeed at and was one of the reasons I went seeking other paths.

Finding Paganism answered some questions and exacerbated others. I was told the Goddess was so vast that she could contain all the different kinds of "women archetypes," that there was a place for me to see myself as holy inside her mirror. But when I looked in the mirror, all I saw was emptiness, negative space where a gender was supposed to be, the outline of what was missing and the parts that still didn't fit. In the god/dess model, there were still only two options, and I didn't really like any of my choices. The thing that was supposed to help me find "freedom" and "empowerment" knocked me back into a two-option prison. And I was still failing, still not understanding the rules, still not fitting the boxes. "Well, if you don't feel comfortable being the goddess, you can be the god!" I was told. I tried that too; it was liberating and fun in the way that a good costume can be. Other parts of me finally had a place where they fit, and that was new. But it still wasn't me. I was still failing at the game I didn't understand the rules to. (And the gods themselves told me, "No, we also cannot be distilled and homogenized like that. Each of us is unique and different. Why would you want to erase our identities, our cultures of origin, all the parts of us that aren't about gender in an effort to simplistically categorize us into a two-box system?" But that is another story for another time.)

I've been a witch and an occultist, a Pagan and a spirit worker for over thirty-eight years. I've been participating in the broader Pagan and polytheist communities since the early 1990s and took my first public oaths as clergy in 1997. About eight years ago, I started an ambitious pan-polytheist learning community called Strong Roots and Wide Branches. The community consisted of monthly classes designed to help participants deepen their polytheist practices. Covering topics including ancestor veneration, building healthy religious communities, land honoring, personal spiritual development, prayer, and many other subjects, the program was geared toward helping polytheists develop healthy and rigorous religious lives.

Ariana was one of my first participants and attended nearly every class for the five years I ran the program. Through her enthusiastic participation in the program, we became friends and co-religionists. We supported one another through developing new religious technologies, co-led rituals, and leaned on one another for peer support as we supported our religious communities as clergy members (and continue to do so). I've attended her rituals and classes; she has participated in my religious side projects.

I've watched Ariana develop her vision of trans-centered polytheist theology over the last number of years, and her work is powerful and righteous.

This is the book I wish someone could have given me when I was in my twenties, struggling to create language that didn't yet exist to try and understand my own heart and show myself to others. This is the road map I wish had been there when I was fumbling through the uncharted wilderness of what I now understand as my own nonbinary, agender identity. I am so glad this book exists now. There are other books that are wonderful for helping guide folks into deepening their understandings of their gender and into accepting who we are. But none of those books are so deeply rooted in a polytheist, animist worldview. Likewise, there are other guides to understanding ourselves from a Pagan or polytheist perspective. But none are centered in a trans worldview. What an incredible gift to have a road map to deeper understandings of Self that rises entirely and unapologetically out of both a trans and a polytheist/animist framework. This book is a blessing.

Who are you? Gender informs the answer to this question, but it is not the entirety of anyone's answer. "Know thyself" is one of the most recognizable and widely known of the Delphic maxims, the first of the three said to have been inscribed upon the pronaos of the Temple of Apollo in Delphi. It isn't possible to know ourselves without further context—identity is contextual, relational: parts of it fixed and static, other parts shifting and dynamic. These are hard questions to answer, and the less we fall into the widest part of the bell curve of identities, the harder it is to even shape language around our understandings and experiences of our own selves.

Who we are is sacred. Who we are is relational and contextual. As Ariana says on page 149, "In knowing yourself, you can know better ways to relate to the world and other people. In knowing yourself, you can find peace between yourself and your fate, and also discern the places where what you may once have thought was fate was instead a distraction or a chain placed on you by others. In knowing yourself, you can be free, and in being free, free to help liberate others too." This is big work, vital work, important work. May your journey through this work be a blessing to you.

River Devora
Founder, Strong Roots and Wide
Branches Learning Community

INTRODUCTION

YEARS AGO WHEN WRITING a column about trans issues, I wrote about personal subjective experiences. What we witness and experience can only be shared by thin threads of language and art; we are lucky when someone else stands up and says, "I've felt that too." Gender is like this: part of one's identity, part of how one moves in society, part of how one is perceived, but mostly and primarily how one experiences their own self. As a person who was newly out as transgender and a person with a lifetime of intense spiritual experiences, it was easy to draw a connection between the two.

In this column, I described how I had been born with a female symbol over my head that nobody but I could see, but I knew that it was there, and it affected everything about my life. Coming out as transgender felt like asking people to take my word on an experience of myself that they had not shared (though to be fair, not many were surprised when I did come out, so it may have been perceived more than I realized at the time). In reality, it is. We know who we are better than the people around us; we know what we experience better than the people around us. There may be a level of subjectivity to these things, but they do objectively affect us all the time.

Each embodied human being has sets of experiences that they cannot share with others directly. Even at the most basic level, we require symbolism created by shared words, images, and other media to help others see what is going on inside our heads, hearts, and bodies.

Even more obscured—occulted, if you will—are spiritual experiences. We can draw an image of the sun and use simple words to describe it: warmth, round, yellow, fiery, hot. The experience of having a spiritual connection to the sun (or one of its gods or spirits) requires an additional level of explanation; it requires embellishment, flourish, technique and, honestly, work to try and help others recognize and understand the experience that you are trying to convey.

If someone has never seen the sun, you could describe it to them. If someone has never spoken to Apollo, you could describe him too. Without the context of having seen or felt the sun, or having encountered Apollo, you will never know if the other person truly understands what you convey.

I am a person who is interested in intense spiritual experiences, being someone who has had a lifetime of them. I've found other people who are similar, and we've shared words and drawn pictures to help one another understand what we are going through. Sometimes even those whose experiences were radically different understood some basic things in common, and sometimes listening to them taught me a great deal about my own life and gave me perspective.

One place gender lives is in the realm of the spiritual, or at the very least, it is a neighbor. It cannot be measured with tape measures or rulers; it has no weight or mass. Yet, like spiritual experiences, its effects on us are massive. Like with spiritual experiences, whole oppressive institutions have grown up around its orthodoxy to punish dissenters or those whose experiences do not line up with the socially approved experiences. In addition, its lack of mass and weight, visible evidence, and easily measurable effects does not mean that it is not very real for those of us experiencing it.

For the modern materialist mindset, that places it in the realm of delusion, something to be ignored or medicated until it is possible to ignore. I do not believe that this has been the standard historic human response to either gender or spirit, and evidence points to broader human understandings of both the ephemeral nature as well as the immanent reality of both of these things. You can't measure a god, but you can certainly measure their effects on your life. You cannot measure your gender, but it absolutely shapes you.

You might think that this was the beginning of my personal exploration of the connection between spirit and gender, but instead it was the first time I had found the language to explain what I had been experiencing. My experiences went back further: in the '90s, as a pseudo-Wiccan, Pagan-type teenager, I had prayed to the goddess to take these feelings away. I asked to stop wishing that I was a girl. I felt her reply that she would do this, but it was something that I would not want.

She was right. I woke up not feeling upset about my gender and how it was perceived for the first time ever. I went through my days, and I realized I didn't feel anything at all. I felt no joy; I felt no sorrow. It felt like a very real and very powerful part of my heart was missing. For a while, I rode this feeling of not-feeling, but eventually it began to feel unnatural. I missed passion and joy and tears, and I was in a gray place where all I did was exist without any actual living. I asked her to reverse it and woke up the next morning with a brilliant panoply of feelings again, a rainbow blooming in my heart and in the sky. I realized that what I had asked her to take away from me was something that was as much a part of me as feeling, as love, as life.

While I was raised in a monotheistic faith, I have had polytheist and Pagan inclinations since I was a small child. Even in that faith, I had experiences connecting the spheres of gender and spirituality (even though spiritual experiences were also something that were tightly controlled and discouraged). As I grew and moved on and became broadly Pagan, I found other ways in which they intersected. I encountered what we called the goddess, and she saw who I was inside. When I was told that "boys" couldn't draw down the moon, I did it anyway, and I felt her in me, and I felt aligned for the first time in my life. I took the part of the goddess in ritual sex. I knew what I was.

My inner spiritual world was a place where I could explore and connect to my gender. While there is definitely a lot of transphobia and gender essentialism in Wicca and broader Paganism, in my personal group of young queerish teens and early twentysomethings, we had not absorbed that and were a bit more play-ful and relaxed when it came to gender. As I grew and eventually became more involved in broader Pagan society, I started to run up against people who made me feel that I needed to hide myself again, even in the context of a spirituality that had allowed my understanding of myself to blossom.

I was mostly closeted for many years, but spiritual experi-ences of and experimentation with gender did not stop and in many ways deepened. My decision to come out, made in 2013, came after a powerful experience walking the labyrinth in Brush-wood, a Pagan campground in New York. My initiation to Kybele happened in relation to my orchiectomy. My choices in spiritual company have always been guided by the openness and gender variance of the people I was approaching. Years of exploring these connections between spirit, the divine, and human understand-ings of gender have left me with a great many thoughts, experi-ences, and practices, many of which I will be sharing in this book.

I write this book as a love song to the dance between spirit and gender. I also write it as a love song to those trans and nonbinary Pagans, polytheists, spirit workers, and others who stand in shared culture and space. I also write it as a manual, a spell book, and a spell to help undo and unbind some of the restrictions around these things that have harmed myself and my people. I also write it to give us tools and tricks, ways of thinking and frameworks and outright magic, to help us build better things for ourselves. It is also meant to be an eye into the overlap between spirit and gender in these spheres.

As a bit of a disclaimer, I am a person of primarily Northwest-ern and Eastern European descent; I'm white. I did not grow up in the so-called United States, but I have lived here most of my adult life. I am aware that there is a vast wealth of knowledge, experience, and power in the gender systems of Indigenous folks around the world, though many of those have been deeply impacted by colonial powers and culture. As the person I am, I cannot write or speak about those genders; that's simply not appropriate. This book focuses on the understanding of gender that has sprung up around transgender and nonbinary people in the English-speaking "Western" world. Likewise, my religious practices are not those of an Indigenous person; I am not the person to speak to the connections between Indigenous spiritualities and their genders. I encourage people to learn from Indigenous people world-round, listen to their speeches, watch their videos, read their books, and, of course, pay them for the hard and dangerous work they do in bringing forth and sharing these things in a world that has been carefully constructed to exclude and marginalize them. I cannot emphasize this enough: white colonial culture has assaulted ancestral connections to sacred expressions of gender not just in Indigenous people but also in people of European descent.

Also, this book proceeds from the idea that transgender and nonbinary people understand themselves. This is not a space where we will be providing arguments for our existence; we exist and always have and always will. Modern politics may rail against us, but that will not stop us from being. I have no interest in defending our right to exist; we have to spend too much of our energy on that already. I'm ready for deeper conversations, as I'm sure many others are.

In fact, a thing I am often reminded of when working with the Trans Dead is that many cultures across the world and across time have known and understood and appreciated folks that we would consider trans or whose experiences are shared with what we understand as transgender and nonbinary people. The current culture of hatred and oppression for those who do not conform to colonial binary gender rules is an aberration in human history—a terrible one, but still, an aberration. We are not the abominations that culture names us; as an integral part of humanity, a culture that names us abominations is in and of itself an aberration and abominable.

People who we would understand as transgender or nonbinary are an intrinsic part of humanity; we have always been, and we always will be. We are a magic born into every human lineage, a reality that speaks to the wholeness of humankind and its connection to the greater world. We have been known as healers, spiritual leaders and guides, workers of magic and wonders, those who speak to the gods and spirits and dead, signs and omens and manifestations of the divine in many places and times. All those things are true in their ways, and also, we are still very human. It is possible to suppress language and expression around our experiences, but that doesn't stop us from having them. It is possible to claim that our understandings and experiences of ourselves are invalid, but that doesn't stop us from being who we are. It is possible to kill us, but not to stop us from being born into humanity, because we are part of it. We are a valuable and integral part of humanity, and a spiritual system that does not accept our existence cannot be truly whole or holy or wholesome.

My people exist, and we deserve to exist. Just as people who are in alignment with their birth-assigned genders see themselves in the divine, so do we deserve to have cosmology that understands the sacred truths that our realities can bring to the table. We are the people of the Mirror, who know ourselves; the people of Mercury, Hermes, and Loki, who shift and change; the people of Dionysos and Aphrodite; the androgynes; the people of Freyja and Frey, of healthy and powerful femininity and masculinity; the people of Phanes, all-gendered firstborn deity; the people of the Serpent, who shed our skins and travel up and down the world tree; the people of Kybele the Mother, of the deepest, original nature, who see the shapes that move beneath the trappings other humans have placed on us, sacrificing the bulls of our restraints to the lions of our natures.[1]

In addition, an understanding of gender and a framework of spirituality that contains and embodies us as well is going to be more holistic and more whole. Whether you are trans or nonbinary or neither, understanding gender beyond the strictly established modern Western binary and incorporating that understanding into your spiritual framework and practices can only be beneficial. Not only will it make transgender and nonbinary people who approach your groups and practices more comfortable and likely to stick around, it will free you from constraints and restraints that are very likely harmful to you and limiting to your practice even if you don't recognize it yet yourself.

I wrote this book with an eye to helping those people who stand in both of these broader communities that I value: transgender and nonbinary communities and Pagan, polytheist, and animist communities. Despite that, I believe this book will be of

---

1. When I capitalize *Mirror*, I am referring to the spirit of the Mirror itself, a spirit I came to know through modern Orphic practice, and one of the sacred Toys of Dionysos.

potential use to anyone with a spiritual practice as well as transgender and nonbinary people whose spirituality feels caught up in restrictive concepts around gender.

"Know thyself" is the most famous of the Delphic maxims, guidelines given by the gods to the Delphic Oracle in ancient times to help guide the path of human life. When you begin to understand yourself, you begin to understand your place in relation to the rest of the world. The prominence of a rigidly enforced gender binary forces most people to view themselves first as men or women, and it forces people to likewise cast that particular filter over the world at large, till everything is categorized in that way. What is *woman* and *man*, and why do we name ourselves these things, and more so, why do we assign these words and related qualities to things like the sun, the earth, the moon, the gods? We have been raised and trained to have this filter and project it onto everything, but I propose that this particular filter obscures more than it reveals, both within and without. Unless it is viewed as optional and other frameworks are considered and brought in, understanding of oneself, one's place in the universe, and the rest of reality are going to be limited by it. I am many things, but among them I am a devotee of Dionysos the Liberator, a path that requires rigorous self-examination and aims at liberation. The chains of enforced, nonconsensual, rigid gender binary are ones that I am happy to take a hammer to as an act of sacred devotion.

I hope that everyone who finds this work will benefit from it. May it help you to see the parts of yourself that have been obscured, may it liberate you from chains that bind you, and may it give you tools to help liberate others.

ONE

WHAT IS GENDER?

THE WORD *GENDER* IS used to describe many different things: sense of self, presentation and appearance, behavior, role in society, and more. What is gender at its core, though?

I want you to take a journey with me. Some of you may have been on a parallel journey. Some may have traveled these waters before, but many haven't, and I think all could benefit from this journey.

Male and *female*, *man* and *woman*, *masculine* and *feminine*: these are the words that come to mind when we talk about gender. So much so that they dominate our conversations about gender. For good reason: Western society has focused so much on these concepts that it's hard to think outside of them at all.

In this work, I hope to give you tips, techniques, and magic to help you look in the Mirror and know who you are and bring that forward into the world. It is only when we know ourselves, our genders, that we can honor them and be in harmony and at peace with them. And it is only when we enact them that we can truly be in alignment with our deepest selves.

Terms, Labels, Names, Taxonomy

I will be using a lot of terms for gender-related stuff in this book. While the intended audience for this work is trans and nonbinary folks, I know that a lot of cisgender people will be reading this book too and may be a bit behind on current terminology.

That being said, current terminology shifts. There are words that were used fairly regularly twenty years ago that are considered slurs or extremely problematic these days. Likewise, there are words that were once considered slurs that have been reclaimed. I also acknowledge that there are going to be shifts that may mean the words I use here will shift in connotation and usage; when further editions happen, I'll update things accordingly. We are going through a massive revolution in our understandings about gender, brought on primarily by ease of access to information and communication, as well as the loosening of laws and restrictions about speaking of these things in some places. There is change, it is constant, and by the time this book reaches the shelves from where I am sitting, typing it out on my computer, some of this may have changed.

Labels are there to help you, not hinder you. Finding that there is terminology that describes who we are can be liberating for people who have never met anyone who expresses those feelings themselves. I'm a late Gen X/elder millennial, depending which way is up, and many of the people in trans support groups I encountered early in my journey were far older than I am. As a teenager, I had internet access and the opportunity to start learning about trans issues from that (as well as from my mother's nursing and psychology books, which were remarkably progressive for being written in the early '90s). A lot of members of the older generation did not have those resources, and one of the refrains that I heard all the time was, "I never knew there was anyone else like me out there."

For someone who has been coping with an aspect of themselves that is reviled and punished by violence, learning that there are other people who feel the same way can be liberating. "You mean I'm not broken, that's a thing? There's a word for that?" is a powerful feeling. It's a feeling that means you are not alone, there are others like you, and if you share nothing else with them, you have at least that. Hopefully there are other living people to help you navigate the complicated path ahead of you that has no pre-established social map (or, at least, not one created by the people affected by it).

At the same time, labels shouldn't restrict you. If you find a label that fits you and you love it and embrace it, that can be a wonderful thing. If it no longer feels like it fits you, it's okay to move on from it (though that can be complicated both internally and in relationship with shared community who uses the same label). Don't let other people try and use a label you love to control you, either. If someone tries to get you to change either what you call yourself or your behavior based on a label that you use, it's their own problem, not yours. The meanings of words are not static, and they adapt to needed use. As long as it is not a culturally specific term, you aren't hurting anyone by calling yourself what you want to (though it may be confusing and require some explanation if folks are used to that term meaning something different).

All that being said, let's talk about terms!

Sex refers to biological traits having to do with reproduction and reproductive capacity. We've been taught the basic version: "male = penis" and "female = vagina," and in high school "male = XY" and "female = XX."

The truth, as always, is more complicated. *Intersex* people exist, folks who are born with a mixture of the great many traits that we assign sex by. They tend to be ignored or treated as an unimportant statistic in the overall discussion and, as children, nonconsensually mutilated to match one of the better-known configurations.

My intent here is not to use the existence of intersex people as some kind of gotcha; it is to help people realize that the existence of intersex categories represents a fault not in intersex people but in our categorization of sex itself, and a fault in the underlying concept. It is also important to respect the dignity and well-being of intersex folks in and of themselves and recognize that while they may have complicated relationships with gender, many do not see themselves as transgender or nonbinary.

Just as with gender, there are exceptions to every supposedly standard bit of morphology or biochemistry that we associate with sex, and those exceptions are far more prevalent than most people are led to believe, partly because many of them are subtle and partly because there is such shame attached to deviation from the stated norms. People who experience these variations often hide them in shame or fear of violence or censure.

People think that sex begins and ends with genitals or chromosomes, but it's far more complex than that. I'll tell you a story by example:

I applied to be part of an HIV study after a representative of a local university came to one of our trans meetings looking for subjects for their studies. I asked them at multiple meetings if any of the treatments a transgender person could have would interfere with the study and was told that it wouldn't be a problem.

I went through the rigorous testing needed for the study and was told that the levels of various chemicals in my blood, particularly hemoglobin, were "off." I was advised to change my diet and try again in a month. I did and had the same results. I spoke with the doctor and asked if they were using male or female ranges for my bloodwork. They said that they were using male ranges because I was "biologically male." I asked them if I fit within the female ranges. I did and had confirmation from my doctor that I didn't have any sorts of health problems that would coincide with abnormalities of those levels.

The representative of the study said, "Well, you know your hormone treatments don't really change anything about your body; you're still genetically male." That prompted a long discussion about biological sex markers. A week later, they called back and said that in future studies, trans people would be considered "biochemically male/female" depending on what form of hormone therapy (if any) they were taking. It was too late for me to join, but I feel like I helped to pave the way for a better understanding on the part of that organization and hopefully others.

So sex has gross anatomical markers like visible genitalia, it has biological markers, it has chemical markers, it has chromosomal markers, and in any one person, those things may not (and frequently do not) align with the supposed "standard" for sex. Quite a few trans people who choose to undergo medical transition have always had some sex markers that were off from what is considered the norm.

In short, sex is a method of categorization that fails when it is used to describe a whole person and should be relegated to necessary medical/biological discussion, if then. At the end of the day, it may be more important to speak about individual components of a person's sex in terms of their actual biology and function.

Also, given that we associate sex with gender assigned at birth, there are a lot of presuppositions about who a person is, what they like, how they behave, and what they are prone to based on this association. Those presuppositions are incorrect at best but are more frequently harmful. Calling someone "biologically male" because you assume that they were born with a penis is not only reductive and unhelpful, but it puts them into a social and biological category with "men" in your brain, whether you mean it to or not, which is incorrect, and the assumptions around it can be deeply harmful when acted on.

This leads us to the next bit of terminology: *assigned gender at birth*. You've probably seen this referred to as "AGAB" and seen the acronyms "AFAB" and "AMAB." Your AGAB is the gender that you were assigned at birth based on what your doctor and parents decided you were due to the shape of your genitals. It is usually something that is referred to in the past tense among trans people; after all, identifying as your assigned gender is literally what being cisgender means (we'll cover that one soon, don't worry!). A person's assigned gender says way more about what other people think about that person than what that person actually is.

Transgender and *cisgender* are two terms used to describe different types of human relationship with assigned gender. The term *transgender* came first. In Latin, it means "across gender" and was originally used for people who are transitioning to a presentation different from the one associated with their AGAB. It is used more broadly now to refer to people who do not identify with their gender assigned at birth, whether they were assigned male and know that they are female, assigned female and know their gender to be fluid and flowing, or any combination thereof. If you do not agree with your birth assignment, you are welcome as part of the transgender umbrella.

People who refer to themselves as *binary* trans people are folks who are transitioning into one of the "two popular genders" (men/women). For instance, a *trans woman* is someone who was assigned male at birth who identifies as a woman, and a *trans man* is a person assigned female at birth who identifies as a man.

Folks who are *nonbinary* do not connect exclusively to one or the other gender. A nonbinary person could be a *demiboy* (partly but not wholly male/man/boy), a *demigirl* (partly but not wholly woman/female/girl), *agender* (not having any felt sense of gender), *genderfluid* (having a gender that shifts by time, circumstance, or both), or others. We have a lot of potential terms for nonbinary identity—far too many to list here—and the language is still evolving. Also, while identities such as agender and *genderqueer* are frequently seen as being part of the nonbinary umbrella, some folks see them as independent understandings of their gender or lack thereof.

Transition is the most common word used to represent the process of internal gender coming to match external expression. People talk about *social transition*, which is all of the social bits of expressing a new gender: new clothes, new hairstyles, new methods of speaking, new pronouns and names, etc.

We also talk about *medical transition*; some transgender people feel the need to change their body through medical intervention as well, for a variety of reasons. Many of us feel a sense of "wrongness" about our bodies the way they are currently set up. That can manifest in different ways, including feeling phantom or energetic sensations of body parts that aren't physically represented, painful feelings or dysphoria (we'll get to that) about current body equipment, and more. A good number of trans people who undergo medical (especially hormonal) transition therapy believe that some of us may have an undetected intersex condition given how much better we tend to feel once we get the right sex hormones. Some people also undergo procedures as part of social transition; they may feel fine about their face or body shape themselves, but they have features that people strongly identify with their AGAB, and that can cause problems socially. Medical transition is not linear, starting with hormones and ending with surgery; instead, think of it as a series of potential options, no one more intrinsically important than another. People are often able to choose what is needed for them. No procedure makes you a particular gender; instead, they are meant to bring your body into alignment with your internal sense of gender. Also, physical transition isn't what makes you trans! Remember, being trans is simply not being in alignment with your birth-assigned gender; what you do about it is a whole other story.

So next we should address *gender dysphoria* and *gender euphoria*. Dysphoria literally translates to "unhappiness." People who experience gender dysphoria have painful feelings about certain things relating to their perceived gender or sexual attributes. Dysphoria is unpleasant; looking in a mirror and seeing something that is absolutely not you can be jarring and painful. Imagine going through your whole life that way! Many trans people do. Dysphoria is not what makes you transgender, but it is definitely a motivation to enact some kind of transition. Cis people sometimes experience gender dysphoria, especially when they are misgendered by strangers for one reason or another, or end up wearing clothes that give them the impression of being from the opposite side of the gender binary and feel uncomfortable about it. Imagine that happens to you for your entire life! That's what so many trans folks go through.

Gender euphoria is the opposite. Trans people speak about gender euphoria most frequently when something happens that makes them feel aligned with their gender and inner sense of self. Wearing clothes that make you feel like yourself, being addressed correctly, getting a new haircut that matches your gender—all of these things can produce euphoria. Many trans people don't experience gender dysphoria, but most of us have experienced euphoria. I consider gender euphoria a reflection of the sacred blessing of bringing yourself into alignment with your true nature.

It's possible to experience both at the same time. I remember being asked once by an X-ray technician if I was pregnant. My shock at being asked was taken instead as uncertainty; grim-faced, the tech said, "Ma'am, if you aren't certain, we can't go through with this." I managed to squeak out, "I don't have a uterus," which ended up confusing him more, but he finally assented, and I got my X-ray.

Euphoria and dysphoria can be guides to understanding yourself. Allowing yourself to feel the push and pull of things that resonate with you versus the things that do not is allowing the deeper currents within yourself to guide you. Listen to your heart, listen to your gut, listen to your spirit and your spirits when it comes to these things. You won't figure it all out at once, but we are all constant works in progress, and if you listen to your instincts and the tides of euphoria and dysphoria, you know that at the very least you will find yourself in the right place for you.

Past, Present, and Future

There is a worldwide revolution of gender occurring right now as a result of many factors: increased access to historical information, improved ease of communication both within and between geographical and cultural regions, and rejection of religious, social, and political narratives (especially those that come from colonizing forces) that seek to define the narrative of gender.

We are in the dawning of it. While historically there have been many places, times, and cultures where transgender people are celebrated, there has never been the widespread ability to connect and discuss these topics freely and cross-culturally to the same extent.

All the terms that are described in this chapter come from that dawning—from this period that is happening as humanity is waking up to a new awareness of itself. I find these terms and concepts useful, and many other people do too. But I will say here as I say elsewhere: this is neither the beginning nor end of this conversation. Our concepts of sex and gender not only can but will continue to be revised over and over through our history and times as we find ways to understand them not just in frameworks isolated by traditions of one group or another, but also by the experiences of individual and groups of humans.

So these words weren't the words we were using one hundred years ago, nor are they likely to be the words being used one hundred years from now as our understandings deepen. That doesn't mean that they aren't valid or useful to folks at this time, but I want to acknowledge and drive home that our current understanding of gender isn't some linear evolutionary pinnacle of thought, but rather, a spot of elevation that tells a broader and *more* complete story, but far from the whole story. I am excited to see what comes next and grateful for what has come before.

We do not have well-formed language yet for a perspective on gender that is entirely disconnected from the two loci of masculine and feminine. This is often used as a reason to invalidate the identities of nonbinary people.

Yet not having a word for something isn't a reason not to believe in its existence. Our languages evolve over time. Colors that there were no words for before did exist before we found a way to distinguish them, and in some languages some of those colors may not have distinct names of their own. Puce is real (at least to our perception, an important point that we will swing back around to), but if you don't have a good mental image for the color, it's just a word. Likewise, if you can see the color in your head but do not have a name for it, it's there all the same, but you may not even consider it its own color. "That's purple-brown," you might think, if that.

Likewise, if you meet a nonbinary person who presents qualities that you associate with masculinity and femininity, you may think of them as "man-woman" or androgynous. You may think of them as "both." But they may instead be something entirely different. Their gender is not based on your perception of their gender.

Another example I love to use is the platypus. Almost universally, people see a platypus and see a chimera, a creature made up of other creatures. A beaver-duck. A platypus is not a beaver-duck; it's not a combination of other animals. It's its own creature, which developed its own shape in reaction to environmental pressures, not impossible crossbreeding. A platypus is whole in and of itself, and so are a great many nonbinary people, who are no more combinations of the two popular genders than our noble monotreme is a combination of waterfowl and rodent outside of metaphor.

The qualities that we ascribe to gender may be innate, but those qualities are not necessarily gendered. High heels are feminine in modern Western culture, but they are descended from the riding shoes of warriors. Dresses were unisex until riding made pants make more sense, and then the people who were more likely to do riding (men) became associated with them. Any single trait that can be named as masculine or feminine can be named as the other (or neither) depending on the culture and time period. There is nothing that is universally associated with one or the other of the two popular genders (even if there are some strong trends).

So the question that we often come back to when exploring nonbinary gender, especially among nonbinary people, is *what is gender, then?* It's clearly not anatomical, since trans men are men and trans women are women, regardless of whatever medical intervention they may or may not have. It's not something innate, though the sense of it can be innate and the qualities associated with it may be innate. What is it?

Gender is many things, and the word can mean many things, but in this work we will be focusing on gender as a form of categorization.

A convention of categorization is not meaningless just because it's not objectively measurable; meaning in the broader sense is far from objective. The qualities ascribed to man and woman, to Virgo and Scorpio, to INFJ and ENTP, may not be measurable by a ruler, but are observable by behavior and interaction. Confirmation bias covers the gaps in observation; social reinforcement by others who also participate in those systems feeds and supports it. Virgos don't get along with Geminis not just because interaction can be difficult for people with certain qualities but because there is buy-in on a personal and cultural level in this belief.

And, in many cases, that buy-in is entirely optional.

What happens when someone doesn't seem to match their natal chart? They say, "Pfft, I don't believe in astrology anyway," to which some will say, "Gee, that's such an X-in-the-Y thing to say," and everyone will nod and get on with their lives. If someone doesn't believe in Myers-Briggs, they may be seen as a killjoy.

What happens when someone doesn't match their ascribed qualities of gender? Social reinforcement. Bullying. Assault. Sexual violence. Social censure. Murder.

The violent enforcement of binary gender makes it no more real or right than the other examples of categorization provided.

I personally long for a world where gendered concepts are treated with the joy with which some treat their fandom's divisions, the curiosity and excitement of pop psychology personality matrices, and the sanctity that some approach astrology with—and the option to opt out that all three have if those systems are not representative.

If you did not use words like *masculine* and *feminine, male* and *female, man* and *woman*, how would you describe your gender? Take a pause and do this exercise.

EXERCISE: WHAT IS MY GENDER?

Get a paper and pen to write or draw with.

Sit in a comfortable position with closed eyes and breathe for a minute to ground and center yourself.

Now, without using the words *masculine, feminine, male, female, man, woman, boy, girl,* or any similarly themed words, describe your gender. What is it? What does it feel like? What is it shaped like? How does it make you feel?

Write or draw whatever comes to mind for your own sense of gender, including if it is nothing or absent. It can be as beautiful and poetic or as short and terse as you like. You're describing a very personal part of yourself: only you know how to express it best.

Most people find this difficult. This set of binary definitions has been used to define everything from body parts to clothing styles to modes of speech to carrots and houses (in languages with binary pronouns, animals and objects are frequently assigned male or female pronouns). However, I've noticed a very particular trend: when I ask this question, the answers that I tend to receive from nonbinary folks are extremely poetic.

"My gender is the sound of the wind in the trees at night."

"My gender is a possum screaming at their own tail."

"My gender is that feeling you get when the coffee wears off, but sometimes it's the feeling that you get when it first hits you. I'm genderfluid, get it?"

"My gender is bees."

Most people who aren't familiar with nonbinary folks will assume that these answers are facetious, and honestly in a few cases they are an attempt to express frustration at a task that's made difficult by the constraints of the system we're taught to think in. Much of the time, though, these answers are an attempt to put words to a feeling. It's poetic self-expression.

My thesis in dealing with gender is that gender identity is an expression of the self. We usually shoehorn it into *man* and *woman* because those are the options that we've been given. When given other options, or when forbidden the standard ones, we find other ways to express it. Those other ways have more and deeper nuance, more flexibility, and may cleave closer to our understanding of our own identities than anything else we've used before.

Identity is what you see in the mirror. Not the bathroom mirror or the compact; it's the Mirror, the spirit-that-reflects, that helps us to know ourselves in the way that the Delphic maxim asks us to.

If identity is what you see in the Mirror, gender presentation is what you do to express that identity.

"Figure out who you are, and do it deliberately"—another maxim, and this one applied to drag, burlesque, and other forms of performance.[2] Forms of performance that are deeply tied to gender and that are self-aware in the understanding that any form of performance is far more powerful if the face behind the mask actually fits the mask itself.

Your gender presentation can be a path to embodiment of your true self, or at very least, it is the category that is used to express it. It is taking what is within that you feel is not represented and making it manifest. We have already established that *man* and *woman* are not the only two options, not by far. There are so many possibilities. If there are things that come up for you that particularly ping as *masculine* or *feminine*, I advise that you think deeply about that and ask yourself what counterexamples exist; if your mind considers makeup feminine, consider the cultures and environments where it has been unisex, for example. You'll realize over time that almost anything that is considered an expression of something masculine or feminine has taken a different role elsewhere, and it is essential that you liberate yourself from the idea that there are inherent cosmic qualities to anything masculine or feminine. It's a lifelong process, and one we all work on, myself included, but it is vital work to do to liberate yourself from the confines of socially enforced gender.

And why does chaining yourself to the confines of socially established gender make this work harder? I believe that you cannot really see the shape of yourself when it is confined by the perceptions of others. While we cannot be entirely free of them, I propose that it is helpful to clean that area of yourself up when

---

2. This quote is commonly attributed to Dolly Parton, though my understanding is that it originated in drag communities.

doing what I call *Mirror work* (work of spiritual self-examination and encountering one's true self). Hold loosely to definitions of specific genders; they are a path to guide you or a coat to warm you and not a wall to obstruct you.

Journaling

I recommend keeping a journal of this work. There are many challenging thoughts and exercises here, and it's valuable to keep track of those things if only to see how our opinions and thoughts change over time.

Go ahead and start one here and now, and just give your impression of what you've read in this chapter. How do you see your own gender? How do other people conceive of and interact with it? Is there a part of yourself, your own identity, that you wish was perceived by others that is not? Is there a part of your own identity that you aren't too sure about and want clarification on?

TWO
GENDER IN PAGANISM AND POLYTHEISM

THERE ARE EXAMPLES OF gender variance both in the history and mythologies of European and Near Eastern polytheism. One would think that transgender and nonbinary people would be welcomed in modern Pagan and polytheist spaces, but often those spaces are not created with us in mind, and as a result are often exclusionary and hostile to us.

Transgender and nonbinary people face discrimination in almost every religious sphere, primarily because religious community and culture always has at least a reflection of the overculture in it, even if it is set up as a foil. In other words, trans people face discrimination in religious spaces because they also face discrimination in public spaces.

This discrimination comes from many places. It is deeply tied into sexism and misogyny and cissexism, and we can talk about each of these.

Sexism is giving preferential treatment to, or discriminating against, one sex over the other. While we may have a more nuanced view of what sex is these days, the way sexism is used most frequently emphasizes the differences in reproductive roles and what is referred to as reproductive labor: people with uteruses are the ones capable of carrying and bearing children, and as such find that a society largely created and policed by cisgender men is one that places undue value on their ability to reproduce. Because reproduction is important for continuation of family line and thus culture and national identity, the patriarchal state exerts tight control over reproductive capacity and often reduces those with birthing-capable bodies to that role, as that role is necessary for its continuation.

Misogyny, on the other hand, is hatred of women or people who are socially coded as women. Misogyny comes from many places. Given that people with birthing-capable bodies are socially required to have children and use their bodies and their labor in childcare for the furtherment of the patriarchal state, attributes associated with people who have birthing-capable bodies—traditionally coded as "women"—are considered attributes of inferiority and weakness. People who are viewed as women are considered intellectually and physically inferior; those who are not seen as women who take on characteristics socially associated with "women" are also considered inferior or somehow sick or defective.

These are premises that I disagree with. The idea that the value of culture and state is high enough that those who are capable of performing reproductive labor should have their lives, identities, and bodies controlled by the state and corresponding culture is where the basis of a lot of discrimination and inequality arise. And lest you think that discrimination or inequality is a "mere" political consideration, this culture is one that encourages people it views as "women" to get pregnant and married as early as possible and to chain their lives to raising children in a particularly socially acceptable way. The culture of sexism and misogyny leads to people prioritizing the continuation of the growth of a fetus over the health, well-being, freedom and, in many cases, life of the birthing parent. It is an attitude that affects the smallest and most mundane of interactions but echoes through the entirety of culture and politics: it is systemic, a pervasive disease.

Western feminism was developed as an attempted antidote and vaccine against these diseases. Feminism has had various movements and modes of thought; it is not a single monolithic thing, nor is it simply quantifiable by its "waves," which often ignore the contributions of women of color and women of non-Western cultures. There have been problems with many forms of discrimination, including racism and ableism, within many feminist movements. The overall goal of feminism, though, is one where people are not controlled by society based on their reproductive roles and where the reductive assignation of personality traits based on those roles or perceived adjacency to those roles have been removed in favor of treating people based on their actions.

The environment of the discussions in (white) feminism that arose in the '60s–'80s was one of the fertile grounds where the seeds of the modern Pagan movement grew and found root. Wicca and other Pagan denominations were seen as a religious field where women could be witnessed as sacred too. Looking to ancient religions that held goddesses in reverence as well as male-coded gods, cultures that had different values with regard to people classically defined as women, and ancient priestesses whose words and deeds commanded respect across the ages, women were able to see themselves reflected in the sacred outside of the meagre offerings that the Christianity of the time provided.

These are powerful and liberatory things, but for a few inherent problems. Too often, history that was found was rewritten to be updated to the mores of the people practicing it. While it would be understandable to allow ancient understandings of feminine divinity to inform modern opinions, outright stating that the ancient opinions matched popular ones is incorrect and doesn't help us learn to do better. If you make your claims based on outright untruths, you should not be surprised if people do not take them seriously.

Another problem was the exclusion of the experiences of women of color and Black women, leading to our current (and in my mind, rightful) backlash against "white feminism," i.e., feminism that centers white women in a society already dominated by whiteness. Excluding women of color and their experiences when they are subject to greater discrimination based on the intersections of racism and sexism is a big problem in modern feminist discourse. Also, white feminism's centering of Western standards of femininity and womanhood has meant the continued exclusion of non-white women in the discussion, continuing even to today.

Cissexism is the assumption that cisgender people are the natural baseline or norm for humanity. It is the idea that people who are classified as *men* and *women* based on their birth assignment are the default and that the behavior we associate with those roles in our society is inherent to people assigned to those roles. This is an unconscious, systemic bias. A person is expected to be cisgender when they are being described in media; a person is assumed to be cisgender before they are born. A culture that prioritizes and considers cisgender people to be primary, natural, and the default automatically classifies people who are not as secondary (if that), unnatural, and bizarre exceptions.

In our current binary system of gender, everything from clothing to choice of career, reproductive role, kind of pen you choose to use (lest we forget the "lady Bic"), types of art and recreation you enjoy—essentially every facet of your life—is based on the physical appearance of your genitals at birth as determined by three people at most. While birth assignment of gender based on genitals may show itself in many cultures, we know that pretty much every facet of person and personality that has been assigned to one gender has been assigned to another in another culture and time.

Transgender People Are Part of Humanity

While the modern understanding of *transgender* is based on modern language and concepts, the core truth remains: among humans there have always been people who do not fit into the narrative that a person's self is defined by their genitals, and there have always been people who did not fit into the gender roles expressed by their society, no matter how expansive they were. The fact is, as far back as we have records of people, we have records of people who we would consider transgender nowadays: from "male" Ancestors buried in "female" attire or fashions, to "women" who claimed and held the identity of "man" and fought for it, to those who were both, neither, or something else entirely.

Transgender people are an inherent part of humanity. Any philosophy or religion that does not account for us—and not just in a particular acceptable manifestation but in all our riotous beauty and power and diversity—does not accept the wholeness of humanity. It leaves out a significant, important, and unrelenting part of the human story. We are a magic born into every human bloodline, a power manifest in human form just as "traditional" concepts of reproductive genders are. We shame the false laws and rules of humanity that say men are this, women are this, and these things are set in stone, and that those lines cannot be crossed, straddled, or ignored entirely. We are as Themis—natural law originating from divine manifestation as opposed to the laws decided upon by humanity. We *are*, and no laws, no cultures, no social mores prevent us from being born into humanity and existing. We will always rise up against those things by our very existence, washing away the tepid presuppositions and artificial manacles humanity uses to control one another. While we may be prescribed against, we appear regardless; while we may be killed, we rise again and again. While attempts are made to erase our existence and narratives, we reject those and reach out across time and distance to reinforce them. We are *eternal*.

A cosmology that doesn't contain trans people is not a human one, and it is not one that can relate to humanity, because it shuns a significant portion of humanity. A theology that sees reproductive men and women as being enshrined as reflections of the creation of the cosmos but doesn't include us *as part of that story* (for whatever reason, people think that we cannot reproduce or

create) is barren and only capable of reproducing stringent bina-
rist thinking and dualistic spiritual coding. If humanity is part of
the story—and all stories we tell have humanity as part of them
in an inherent fashion—and we are not part of the story, then
that humanity is stunted, weak, and ultimately incomplete. We
are part of human completeness; we belong, we are inherent, and
as long as there are humans, so we will be.

In Pagan Spaces

So you can imagine how many modern trans and nonbinary folks,
either encountering Paganism or polytheist practice or coming
into this understanding of themselves while being engaged in it,
might feel left out. Much of the culture and language of modern
Paganism arose out of a feminist movement that intended to liberate but utterly failed many of the people who needed its help the
most, and those ideas have ossified and become baked into it. In
addition, modern Pagan and polytheist movements arise out of
an overculture that does its best to try and vilify, mock, and ultimately erase transgender and nonbinary people. The cissexist ideals of European-based colonial culture are also deeply inscribed
on many of the assumptions in practice and dogma.

In many cases, this is not by design. Systemic forms of oppression and discrimination remain systemic because the systems that
uphold them aren't living and distinct things, rather they are per-
nicious diseases upon culture and society. Cissexism is pervasive;
it is part of our language and our society, and it's hard to see it
when we are always surrounded by it. It takes being brought to
awareness of cissexism to identify it, to consider ways to counter

it, and to find healthy ways of moving forward—holistic ways of being that include trans people as a full part of humanity instead of treating us as incomplete, sick, or monstrous.

For instance, a transgender person wanders into a Heathen ritual and the Goði, or priest, is calling on the Ancestors and speaks specifically of "the Alfar and Disir" and translates them to "Male and Female Ancestors" (which is arguably an incorrect attribution in the first place: those terms were used to describe different types of beings in different places and times). The transgender person then knows that this community doesn't make space for someone who is neither, or that this community names its dead by the shapes of their genitals. A nonbinary person wants to come out to their coven, but the ritual language that they use speaks of a single goddess and god from whom all things come and to whom all things return, and they know in their heart if they come out, they will be told that their body is of the goddess because they have a uterus, when they know that neither role fits them. A polytheist sees a transfeminine goddess in a vision of Freyja, and they are told by their community that it is obviously Loki, who is the "only trans deity," as though concepts of current, mortal, cultural gender define the powerful spirits and beings that carry the energies of cosmic forces. All of these experiences are real-life examples and harmful even if the harm is not deliberate.

Intent and action are not the same. If someone does not intend to break a plate or run someone over and yet drops the plate or has an accident, the plate is still broken and the other person is still injured, regardless of the intent. While intent is important as guidance, it doesn't define whether or not an action is harmful and certainly doesn't define whether or not someone has been harmed.

"I didn't mean to" isn't the same thing as "I didn't do it." Doing harm by accident does not absolve you of responsibility for that harm.

Transgender and nonbinary people have felt excluded in Pagan and polytheist spaces since these spaces began to manifest in what we consider the modern era. While there are exceptions, even in those cases the theology or ritual language or practice was somehow stretched to fit them in a way that did not serve the wholeness of the spiritual narrative or the person that was being encompassed—especially as those alterations have often been based on a cisgender understanding of transgender identity.

If trans people are to be welcome as part of Pagan and polytheist culture and traditions, then those traditions must incorporate an understanding of gender that includes them from the very beginning, not as outsiders for whom the blanket must be stretched out of shape.

In fact, many of the mythologies and histories that inspire modern polytheist practices and modalities have ample qualities that can lend themselves to opposing cissexist thought, even if that was not the original intent. Additionally, most of these themes came from societies that already had different understandings and ways of dealing with concepts of gender and reproduction and human identity. They are already being stretched to fit modern overculture in a way that is pleasing to their practitioners. If you are already going to be adapting things to fit the way that you see the world, it isn't hard to adapt them in ways that are liberatory and supportive of marginalized people. Revelation and religion and spirituality happens now; even reconstructionists generally admit that living religion is something that is not static and that the past may inform their practice and belief but is not a stone wall or steel chain meant to violently shape it.

If your spiritual practice—if your Paganism or polytheism—cannot include trans and nonbinary people, then it cannot be whole or healthy; it cannot account for an inherent part of human nature. On the other hand, there is no reason not to have an understanding of your cosmology that is inclusive from its basis, other than the hard work of changing your preconceived notions about these things, and that hard work is always richly rewarded by spirit and community alike.

Specific Trends

There are specific trends that I am interested in addressing with regard to Pagan and polytheist practice and culture that I feel cannot be ignored in a book about sacred gender that centers transgender people. These are some of the things that tell transgender people, "You are not welcome here. At best, we don't understand you and don't care if you don't fit into our concept of the sacred; at worst, we actively want to exclude you."

The Triple Goddess

I know this cuts to the heart of the practice of many Pagans and thus may be a hard one to hear about, but it is central to some of these issues. The triple goddess, as we currently recognize it in the structure of Maiden-Mother-Crone, is a concept developed whole cloth by Robert Graves and yet has been carried through into modern polytheist practice to a degree that is both depressing and alarming.[3]

First, let me say: there are many triple goddesses. There are goddesses who appear as a collective (such as with the Matronae, the Norns, the Moirae, and others), who appear to have three faces or bodies (such as with Hekate), who seem to typify various aspects of a single goddess (Brighid and the three Brighids), or who are similar related goddesses who hold a title (as with the Morrigna: Anand/The Morrigan, Badb, Macha; and occasionally others). There are others who defy neat classification who also exist in European mythology. That being said, none of them are tied to the concept of Maiden-Mother-Crone that was developed by Robert Graves. We should remember that Graves was not a practicing polytheist, and his work is broadly denounced by modern historians of all genders as being pseudohistorical or ahistorical, nor was he in any way a feminist or measurably liberatory toward women and reproductive labor in comparison with other authors of the time. There is no one single theme with goddesses that appear in triplicate, tripartite, or as three-part collectives, much less one based on reproductive role.

Limiting the role of a powerful and sovereign deity or deity collective to stereotyped representations of reproductive roles is reductive and diminishing. Organizing the "divine feminine" to three stages of life corresponding with prepubescence, fertility, and menopause simply reaffirms the view that people who are capable of bearing children are (a) women and (b) defined by their

---

3. Mark Carter, *Stalking the Goddess* (Alresford, UK: Moon Books, 2012), 4, 294, 319–22.

ability to and relationship with bearing children. This is incorrect on all fronts. Women are so much more than their ability to have children, and so many women—cisgender and transgender alike—are, for many reasons, infertile. Fertility of the womb is not a measure of the value of a human being in any society but a patriarchal one. (And in patriarchal societies, the value of people with wombs is often tied primarily to their ability to reproduce.) In addition, there are many people capable of giving birth who aren't women: there are many trans men, transmasculine people, and nonbinary people with uteruses who are capable of giving birth.

While I understand that this framework is a well-established one, it is one that has been founded on false ideas about gender, reproduction, life cycles, and ancient mythology and theology. From a historical perspective it is glaringly incorrect, from any perspective it is patriarchal, from a trans perspective it is deeply alienating.

There are many ways to represent and explore a deity in triplicate aspects without delving into historically inaccurate biological essentialism. If we want to speak about phases of life, we can speak about "Learning, Assimilating, and Disseminating" phases, about "Youth, Adulthood, and Elder" status. Or you could, in fact, speak to different reproductive phases without using an inherently transphobic and cissexist framing, i.e., one that ties reproduction to gender without using gendered language that is othering and, again, sets up the cosmos as one where trans people are aberrations and exceptions rather than a working and living part of it.

"Women's" Mysteries

Private spiritual rites affirming the spiritual nature of women, connecting them to their divine matrons, spirits, and selves, empowering them magically and deepening their inherent, embodied connection to womanhood—what could possibly be wrong with that?

Nothing, not a single thing. I am in support of all sorts of Mystery religion (I have been a priestess in one, after all). Often, when we talk of Mysteries, what is being referred to is a shared sacred, intuitive understanding of an experience, the transformations that occur in relationship with that understanding, and the rites that convey that understanding. Mysteries can't be written out on paper or just spoken with words; real Mysteries must be understood, internalized, and connected to on a gnostic (intuitive spiritual wisdom) level.

It is definitely possible to have Mystery rites, practices, and groups centering women and women's experiences. It is also possible to have similar rites and practices surrounding reproductive status. The problem is when the two are conflated.

A uterus does not make you a woman. Menstruating does not make you a woman. There are many people with those parts and experiences who are not women, and those people often feel alienated by their implicit inclusion in "Women's" Mysteries, which are usually Mysteries surrounding uterine reproductive qualities and experiences.

Not having a uterus, never having had a uterus, does not mean that you are not a woman, either. There are women who are assigned female at birth who are born without uteruses, and there are trans women who are born without uteruses. Stating that a ritual is for

"Women's" Mysteries and then excluding people without a uterus (and it only ever ends up being trans women, not cis women who had differently developed reproductive anatomy or who have had hysterectomies) is also something that is based on a misunderstanding of the relationship between gender and reproductive anatomy.

It would be easy to rebrand the rites and practices surrounding these particular reproductive Mysteries as "Uterine" Mysteries, "Menstrual" Mysteries, etc. without the blanket misgendering of so many trans people (trans men and nonbinary folks who have uteruses being called "women" for this purpose, trans women being considered "men" for this purpose). It is also possible to have Women's Mysteries that focus on actual womanhood and shared experiences of women rather than shared reproductive experiences (which women, including cisgender women, do not universally share).

Trans women and nonbinary women can provide a unique perspective on the experiences and spirituality of women. Trans men and nonbinary people with uteruses can provide a unique perspective on the experiences of people with that anatomy through the eyes of another gender (and trans men have a lot of amazing insight into manhood!). Simple attention paid to the language and concepts behind these things will not only end up making your spaces and rites more inclusive, they will also bring in powerful richness and diversity of experience and new and exciting forms of connection between people, as well as new avenues of spiritual connection. Nothing is lost by doing this; there are only benefits to be gained for all.

Masculine and Feminine Divine

While there have always been deities identified as female or feminine, the rise of the language around the "feminine divine" in a Pagan context is directly tied to the reaction against an overculture that assumed the overgod was male. It makes absolute sense to counter that with, "Women are divine too; divinity also includes the attributes that we associate with womanhood and femininity." It also makes sense to elevate the spiritual aspects of birthing and bodies that are capable of it, given the long history in Christianity of degrading these natural functions and seeing them as unclean.

The problem comes, again, with the conflation of gender and gendered categories with bodily functions (which the language around biological sex still overwhelmingly falls into). I understand that at the time much of the religious language around the "divine feminine" was developing, there was not as much dialogue around gender variance and trans identity (in fact, second-wave feminism is famously hostile to trans people, especially transgender women). At this point, though, we know better, and we know more and discuss this more every day. A religion or spiritual model that does not adapt to human understanding of experiences, that refuses to acknowledge science, is not one that is going to survive in any sort of healthy way, and this has shown itself time and time again in the ways that the language around the "divine feminine" has been weaponized against trans men, trans women, and nonbinary people of all varieties.

I fully support finding divine connection in gender; this is something I and a great many trans people do. I also fully support efforts to sacralize the reproductive functions of bodies that have for too long been deemed unclean or unhealthy. Bodies are sacred; reproductive functions can be sacred; genders can be sacred too. Bodies are sacred whether they are used for pregnancy or not. Femininity can be sacred for those who connect to divinity that way.

These two things are separate things. So many trans and nonbinary people I speak to who have a uterus (or are assumed to) are leery of interacting with Pagan and polytheist groups because of the repeated ideas that their wombs are what makes them sacred, all couched in language that defines them as "women" in the face of who they really are. So very many trans women I know refuse to associate with other Pagans and polytheist groups because they've been told that they are men and will always be men, that their "energy" is "male energy," and that they don't have wombs and therefore can only represent the divine masculine. (Cis women without wombs are told that they have "astral wombs" and that trans women do not, to which I have two counters: first, many trans people experience phantom or energetic experiences of body parts, especially reproductive organs, that they do not physically have, and second, there never seems to be an "astral OBGYN" to check on the status of a person's astral womb.) This kind of language is an attempt to control the lives and narratives of trans people and force them into roles that they are not fit for.

Why does divinity need to be gendered? Especially if your concept of the "divine" is more pantheistic (as it is in many witchcraft spaces), something that dwells in and connects to all things, there is no need to split it into what we have established are arbitrary human categories, especially when coupled with the biological essentialism connecting them to genitalia. Even if you do choose to acknowledge a divine feminine and masculine in your practice, you are clearly leaving something out of the equation if you do not take into account energies that do not fit neatly into those categories. And there is no way to base a person's entire spiritual reality around the genitals that they presented at birth without being grossly reductive; again, this reinforces patriarchy instead of working toward its abolition.

"Masculine" and "feminine" attributes have long been used in various magical systems, but the idea that the people who developed those systems and understandings had no concept of the existence of what we know of as trans and nonbinary people is completely unfounded. Even if it were true, we exist in defiance at attempts to narrow us down and control us; we will not be stopped from being who we are, and we are a natural part of humanity and the world. These systems can adapt to our existence, and the language around them can adapt too; our language used for spiritual work and practice changes all the time. Spirituality is living; it flows like water and like light, and when it is trapped, it slowly dies and ossifies into tools of social control rather than sacred connection to the universe.

Trans women are women, trans men are men, and nonbinary people are both, neither, or some shade of the two. We are who we say we are, and a concept of the divine that places us as unnatural or outright states that our understandings of ourselves are incorrect is a concept of the divine that is in and of itself incorrect—a shattered and broken reflection of a whole, wholesome, and holy tapestry of creation.

I can't complete this section without also stating that there are other religious forms that incorporate concepts of divine masculine and feminine—for example, the branch of Hinduism known as Shaktism (whose teachings are often misappropriated by white Westerners who don't have full context for them). The irony is that Shaktism is non-dualistic, and by word of some modern practitioners, nonbinary. Using concepts from healthy, ancient religious traditions to reinforce bigotry in a culture that they did not spring from is both appropriative and sacrilegious.

Doing Better

So how can you do better? What can you do to make spaces more inclusive to trans and nonbinary folks? We have already talked about how these gender-essentialist ideas are harmful to trans folks, and also how they reinforce patriarchal ideals that in the end are harmful to cis people as well. And I reiterate: trans people are part of humanity; any spirituality that others us leaves out a portion of the human story and is incomplete and flawed. There are many reasons to revise how you approach gender in your practice.

With an eye toward being more inclusive and having a healthier spiritual practice and cosmology, how do we incorporate an understanding of spirituality that doesn't depend on the gender binary and genital-based gender essentialism? I have a lot of ideas and suggestions. These are meant to be suggestions, guidelines, and ideas, and the beginning of a discussion but far from the final word.

First off, let transgender and nonbinary people speak to and define our own space and roles in the cosmos. Let transgender people define themselves. The urge to force trans people into a particular spiritual narrative is one that comes from a place of domination and cultural hegemony. If you are not one of us, you do not understand us and how we understand ourselves. If you do not understand the ways that we understand ourselves, then how can you be sure that you are right in deciding that trans people "are a mix of female and male energies" or "are a particular combination of these soul parts" or "have this particular past life or soul back-story" or any of the great many other assumptions trans people need to put up with? Many ideas like this come from a cisgender person hearing one trans person's narrative for themselves and then projecting it across us collectively in ways that are harmful, even when they come from a place of good intention.

If you want to understand how trans people should be seen in relation to the gods and spirits of your spiritual tradition or path, listen to the trans people in that tradition or on that path. Trust me, we know ourselves better than you could. (If there are no other visible trans or nonbinary people in your tradition, that in and of itself should be a huge red flag; why aren't they there? Trans folks are everywhere, and if you don't see us it's either because we know we don't belong in a space or because those of us who are there are too tired of being shouted down when we speak up.) Regardless, talk to trans people who are part of your tradition. If there are no clergy that are transgender, speak to non-clergy (and again, if there are no clergy who are openly trans, there's probably a reason and it's probably not a good one).

Second, interrogate the language and assumptions that you make in regard to reproduction. So much of the transphobia and cissexism in Paganism could easily be countered if this were done. Connecting concepts of gender, performance, expression, and spiritual role with reproductive anatomy is where many of these ideas begin. Decouple these things in your mind, in your words, in your practice. The goddess can have a womb without a womb being the distinguishing characteristic of a goddess. What are you trying to talk about when you are talking about her womb? Is it her capacity to create? That's something all humans have. Is it part of her role as a purifier/recycler of souls (as with the Chaldean Hekate Soteira)?[4] That is a process that doesn't need to have gender associated with it either. Are you talking about things being receptive and projective? If so, why are you attaching the language of "masculine" and feminine" to those things when you know that to be masculine does not mean to be "projective" and feminine does not mean to be "receptive"? How about, instead, just calling them "projective" and "receptive"?

Remember when I asked you to think about your gender in terms outside of *male/female, man/woman, boy/girl, masculine/feminine*, etc.? Do that any time that language comes up in your spiritual practice. Ask what you really mean with that language. Once you find a way to express what you really mean, say that instead! It may feel awkward and clunky at first, but the precision will be beneficial to everyone involved. And, if you really mean masculine and feminine, interrogate what those things mean to you in the context of this practice.

Third, make room for more than two. When we talk about deconstructing or fighting the binary, we are generally not saying that this pairing should not exist; it's a reminder that it's not the entire story, and the parts of the universe that are nonbinary and do not fit into that neat little schema far outnumber the ones that

---

4. Sarah Iles Johnston, *Hekate Soteira: A Study of Hekate's Role in the Chaldean Oracles and Related Literature* (Atlanta, GA: Scholar Press, 1990), n.p.

do. The world cannot neatly be divided into two, or even three, four, or more. It is entirely possible to work with *polarities* without claiming that those polarities define all of existence; that's incorrect and irresponsible, and on the human level cuts so many people out of alignment with the sacred cosmos. Light and dark define one another, and with them come various shades of twilight and dawn, and yet there are things that are not well categorized by light, dark, or the shades between. Remember, a useful way to look at gender is as a form of categorization, and while categorization is helpful, it is not intrinsic or absolute; it is our method of interacting with a deeply complex universe that we can only perceive a tiny portion of. Play with that categorization and recognize it as a sacred Toy or tool. It is helpful for certain practices and contexts, but in the end, focusing on it is a distraction, as the goal is not the Toy or tool; it is the project or game being worked on or played with it.

Fourth, trust trans people when they see themselves in something. Whether it's an Ancestor, a deity, a natural feature, or an energy, if a transgender or nonbinary person looks at something and says, "That resonates with me; that's trans," listen to them. You may not see it; you probably won't. That's okay because we don't always see your binary categorizations either. Seeing the transgender or nonbinary nature of something sacred is an expression of sacred connection for transgender and nonbinary people. If you don't agree, try to understand, and if you can't understand, simply be quiet and let us do religion and spirituality the way that works for us. Acknowledge that different views of these things can be healthy and that there are parts of these pictures that you cannot see because of who you are, as we are all limited by our perceptions and experiences even as we strive to overcome those things. If you think referring to a deity or Ancestor as trans or nonbinary is insulting, you have some transphobia of your own to work through. When a trans person says a god or Ancestor was trans, *listen* and *don't argue.* You may learn something about that being, about spirit, or about yourself in the process, and again, everyone stands to gain here.

Fifth, remember that trans and nonbinary people understand our own relationship to gender better than you do. Mysteries cannot be explained; they have to be lived. If you have not lived these Mysteries, then you do not understand them. If you have lived these Mysteries and someone else has also and you do not agree on them, it is likely because they have a different set of experiences than you. I don't know what it's like to be a trans man. I can guess from what friends and loves have told me, but I will never know what it is like to look out through eyes that have gone through what they have gone through. I'm not going to gainsay them their understanding of spirit and gender so long as they aren't applying it to other people.

At the end of the day, listen to us, and if you have any power or influence in your group or tradition, work to implement the changes we need to be able to be part of it. That's the place this starts and ends; the rest is just details.

Journaling

What have your experiences regarding gender in Pagan spaces (online and in person) been like?

If you are cisgender, have you witnessed trans and nonbinary people in your spaces? What have their experiences been like and why?

If you are transgender or nonbinary, what ways have you felt left out, not perceived, or excluded from Pagan and polytheist spaces and writings? Where have you felt affirmed and supported by them?

In the cosmology of Pagan groups, spaces, and writings, how have you seen gender treated? Think of an example that you consider harmful and think of an example that you consider wholesome or affirming.

How does your cosmology include and represent transgender and nonbinary people and ideas?

THREE

GENDER AND
THE DEAD

A UNIVERSAL TRUTH OF humanity is that death comes to us all and no one escapes it. On a spiritual level, this also means that it is part of humanity and being human. Those who have come before and died also had their own connection to and understanding of gender, and learning about them and engaging them spiritually can help one navigate one's own gender.

The modern Paganism that I was exposed to in my youth in the '90s did not emphasize working with or connecting to the dead. In fact, most of the Pagans and witches that I met had one of three potential responses to dealing with the dead: (1) to treat the spirits of the dead as terrifying things to be banished or forced to "move on," (2) to claim that working with the dead brought you closer to death and thus would lead to an early death, and (3) to claim that working with the dead was impossible because of reincarnation. (No surprise, most of those Pagans were white folks with limited exposure to other cultures; at the same time, most of them were doing their best with the materials that they had available).

Over time, the issues in these worldviews became apparent. Not all of the restless dead want to move on, and they are certainly not all hostile. If working with the dead brings you an early death, then the majority of human cultures through history that practice or have practiced forms of ancestor veneration must be bucking that trend. Also, there are plenty of spiritual paths that work with both reincarnation and ancestor veneration; this is often approached through the idea of a multipart soul or the idea that reincarnation isn't something that happens to every single spirit every single time.

My personal spiritual community discussed these things, and over time, we became aware of the ahistorical quality of these ideas. The more we discussed and considered, the more it became apparent that not connecting to the Ancestors in any way meant we were missing out, and the others and I began examining these connections and began to work more deeply with them, starting with offering to them and finding other ways to connect.

I still remained leery of the dead for a long time, however, despite trying to take baby steps to support them. The two things that changed that were coming out as trans and finding supportive community to help with learning actual techniques for connecting to the Ancestors.

The year that I came out as trans was a magical year. I was spending time at the Sirius Rising festival at Brushwood (a spiritual campground in upstate New York), where there is a lovely cairn made for ancestor veneration in the middle of a field surrounded by tall grass. I had made the decision to come out a few days before in the festival, and I knew that I needed all the spiritual support I could find. I came to the ancestor cairn in the dead of night, under the brilliant stars that seemed so close to my head at that elevation, and prayed. I asked for those who had come before me, who had undertaken this or a similar journey, to come forward and help me. The air twinkled with fireflies as I prayed—stars above in the sky, stars surrounding me in the air, stars blinking on the ground in the grass.

After my prayer, I stood in the darkness, waiting, but not sure for what. Silently, a form rose out of the ground in the dark, a humanoid shape, and as it rose, it stepped to the side, pulling something else with it. The shape was holding the hand of another shadowy form, helping to pull it up out of the ground. This continued in a sequence as a chain of spirits, like paper dolls linked at the hands and made of shadow (though of different sizes and shapes), pulled themselves out of the darkness and surrounded me.

I was terrified. I was in awe. And I felt oddly safe. I thanked them and repeated my prayer.

One from the group stepped forward to speak to me. We communed, and through her I felt the love, the support, and the connection with the Trans Dead. She stayed with me as a spirit guide for many years, helping me through rough spots in my transition. She came from a time and place and people where folks like us were known and seen as holy, and the most important message that she carried to me was this: our current culture that hates and fears trans folks is an exception and a mistake. There are many times and places in human history where our people have been loved, upraised, and celebrated, and there are many lives of folks just like us that have been filled with the joys and love and understanding of worth that were afforded to any member of their society. Her reminder was that we are loved and have been loved and honored and respected. Despite the fact that modern culture does its best to erase us and our histories, we are part of history, part of humanity, part of the present and the future, and we matter as part of the human story. The current aberration of transphobia is just that: an aberration in human history. Once we were loved and honored and respected, and implicit in that message is that we can be, and we will be, again.

Thank you for the lessons, friend. I will never forget you.

What Is Ancestor Veneration?

Ancestor veneration is one of the oldest recorded forms of human spiritual practice, possibly even predating other religious concepts. It is something that exists in many forms in multiple practices and seems to be a baseline of human spirituality, with the paths that reject it outright being in the minority.

It is what it sounds like: honoring those who came before you, who brought you life and helped you to become the person that you are today.

Why would you engage in ancestor veneration?

There are quite a few factors that work their way into this. Before I get started, let's start with some baseline assumptions that build into ancestor work:

1. Dead people continue to exist in some fashion.

2. Dead people can hear the living and can communicate with us in some way.

3. Dead people, like living people, care about their lineage and what comes after them, and they care to some extent about the things that they cared about in life.

4. The Ancestors are willing to help you. Collectively, they want to see you do well.

These assumptions are far from unusual in human spiritual practice; indeed, spiritual practices that don't incorporate these ideas are far less common through human history.

So why would you engage in ancestor veneration?

At a basic biological level, practice of gratitude is helpful for your mental health, and gratitude is central to ancestor veneration practice.

Honoring those who came before you helps to place you in continuity and context. Modern society so often severs us from our roots as well as our branches, imagining humans to be individuals without precedent or antecedent. Connecting with Ancestors who shared aspects of your life can help you to feel less alone and more loved and connected to humanity as a whole, and help you to understand that there are, and have always been, people like you.

When I teach about ancestor work, I sometimes like to say, "Just because she's dead doesn't mean Grandma can't give you twenty bucks when you need it." The dead care about you, individually and collectively, and are very good at helping with the practical, human-level work of day-to-day life. They have also eaten and drank and pissed and shat, danced and sang and gotten sick and depressed, paid taxes and dealt with bureaucracy, found sublime spiritual and sacred connection to the gods and divine. They've been through it, and no spiritual power has the same grounded connection to the world that the dead do.

Not only can they help with practical daily miracles, their existence as living humans allows them a perspective and experience that is deeply valuable; asking them for knowledge or understanding or wisdom about a subject can lead you to interesting thoughts, revelations, and blessed guidance.

Many people believe that offering to the dead, remembering them, saying prayers for them, lighting candles for them, and other practices we perform, helps to support them in their afterlife. When you die, wouldn't it be nice if someone thought about you as well and sent you things that would be helpful for you?

If you are trying to connect to anything that is an aspect of human life in any way, you have Ancestors who have tried to do the same or a very similar thing.

If you do any sort of work with ancient deities, you know that we frequently have a small amount of information to go on about them because of loss of language, texts, and culture for many reasons (but primarily colonialism and imperialism). Lacking other sources, praying to the dead who honored them is valuable because they can provide us with guidance and insight in connecting to, understanding, and being in right relationship with these powers whose traditions have been lost or deliberately erased.

I'd also like to draw a distinction between *ancestor veneration* and *hero worship* (and here I'm not using that term with any sort of value judgment). *Ancestor veneration* is generally a collective practice of reaching out to your Ancestors in general—or groups of them in general, and possibly individuals like known family members—but still acknowledging them as part of a whole or collective of those who were human and have moved on from that state.

Hero worship, on the other hand, is working specifically with those beings that many Pagans call the Mighty Dead or the Glorious Dead—beings who may once have been human but through memory, worship, and broad acknowledgment have been raised to a higher level than other humans in a spiritual sense (not unlike Catholic saints, though often with a far less formal practice). They often have power, resources, and connections that are different from other dead humans, and in some cases may be considered to be humans who have achieved some level of divinity (such as with Antinous).

Both of these are specific ways to work with Ancestors, and both of them are valuable to the work that is presented here. Collective ancestor veneration, along with speaking to specific Ancestors, is valuable for connecting to lineage and finding collective identity, and work with gender is work with identity. On the other hand, hero worship is useful for those who feel especially inspired and guided by a particular well-known, historically attested, or mythologically named dead person. Both are useful tools and have roots in the oldest human spiritual practices.

However, ancestor work is often complicated for modern folks, especially those who recognize actions of individual, harmful Ancestors. So I feel it's a good time to address that before moving forward.

Your racist Uncle Bob is one human in a vast stream of humans stretching back two hundred to three hundred thousand years. We have only been writing about our own history for five thousand years; that's less than 5 percent of the time that human beings have been being human. When you call on the Ancestors in general, you are calling on all of them, and while individual humans may have been harmful to you or done terrible things, the vast force of humanity—all the people who led up to and contributed to you being alive—isn't a terrible thing. I know that because they created you, and you are not a terrible thing. When we reach out to Ancestors collectively, we are asking them to look past individual wrongdoing and prejudice and help their child in need, and even if your own parents did not show you love, there are humans who have passed from this world that you are descended from by blood or by inspiration or by lineage that do care. Your Ancestors, individually, may have been complicated people. Your Ancestors, collectively, want to see you do well, be healthy, be prosperous, and have good things. You are the living part of them, their living representative, and humans generally care for their children. You are their child no matter how old you are.

I'm not going to get terribly deep into different techniques for ancestor work in this book, but given that Western society is one of those cultures that has (in many cases deliberately) separated us from the human birthright of having a good relationship with our Ancestors, I'm going to give a few basic starting tips. Feel free to use them or not; if you don't, I recommend you research the same subject in other directions. The Ancestors are here, they are real, and they want to help. If you reach out to them, they will come running to you.

BASIC ANCESTOR PRACTICE EXERCISE: TALKING TO THE STARS

Stars also play a powerful part in ancient human spirituality, and the connection between the stars and the dead cannot be underscored enough. There are many associations in mythology and culture between the stars and the dead, from the belief that the stars contain reflections of us or reflect the will of the gods in our world, leading to sacred arts like astrology, to the fairly widespread belief about people becoming stars after they die, to the apotheosis myths of Dionysos where he raises people up to become constellations, Starry, or divine.

When I first became interested in working with the dead, I approached Freyja in her aspect as Valfreyja, "Lady of the Slain," and asked her for help moving into a practice I was very nervous about. What follows is a version of what she gave me in meditation.

Go outside on a night when you can see the stars. Take a good look at the sky and get a feel for the stars around you.

Think about a person who has passed on that you wish you could talk to right now.

Pick a star. Any star. It doesn't matter if you forget which star it is. It doesn't matter for the purpose of this practice if the star already has another name or significance. Simply pick a star.

While looking at the star, start saying the things to the deceased person you want to speak to. Pour your heart out to them; share what you want to say to them. Treat the star as though it is that person, just for this moment, just for the purpose of having somewhere sacred to direct your prayers.

Once you are done talking to that person, take a pause. Breathe, listen, think, and see if you get any impressions or feelings you didn't before. You aren't wrong if you don't; that's not the purpose of the exercise. Here, we are just reaching out.

Think of another person who has passed on that you wish you could communicate with. Pick another star. If there are a lot of stars and you pick the same one by accident, it's okay. Seriously, don't worry about that. Just pick a star, call it by that person's name, talk to it, and listen.

That's it; that's all. We are just here to start; we don't need to do anything complicated or fancy. Ancestor work, at its base, does not need to be complicated or fancy. By connecting with the dead, you are engaging with your human birthright and bridging the gap between now and eternity, between you and greater things, and between the living and the dead.

Trans and Nonbinary Ancestors

Now that I've spoken about how binary gender—man and woman, male and female—are constructs, let me let you in on something else: they're also real.

Something being constructed doesn't mean that it isn't real; indeed, that's what construction is: building and creating something. We have established and created these systems of gender already, and as we've discussed, we know that they vary by place and time and culture.

This is where the Ancestors come in.

It is very likely that if you are reading this and had more than one parent, one of your parents identified as a woman and probably as your mother. In most cultures in the world, the pairing of man and woman as parents is a default and an expectation.

One of your mother's parents probably identified as a woman. So did many of your Ancestors, stretching way back in time. As I like to remind people when we get into ancestral work, humans have been human-ing for close to 300,000 years. We've only been writing about it for five thousand of those years. Less than 5 percent of human history is what we consider "history." When it comes to Ancestors and ancestor work, not all of them are your blood kin, either. Any lineage that you are part of has its Ancestors.

You have thousands of generations of women and men before you. If *woman* or *man* appeals to you, regardless of your birth assignment, you not only have a pre-generated gender available to you, but spiritually you have an obvious lineage of Ancestors you belong to. People have been teaching people the guidelines of performing those roles for a long time (a process a lot of trans folks feel left out of due to being assigned and forced into the wrong gender). You have lineage; you have Ancestors of Womanhood or Manhood behind you that you can call on in need, honor in gratitude, and emulate in reverence and joy.

Manhood and womanhood are powerful constructs, and many people find joy in them. They can also be harmful constructs because the general understanding of them actually fully fits very few people; one-size-fits-all usually means everyone-is-at-least-a-little-unhappy-and-many-are-in-pain. This is because they are enforced based on the outward appearance of the genitals that an infant is born with, and often enforced violently. Oppression seeks to replicate itself to provide power to oppressors, whether or not those oppressors are aware of it. (And if a baby's genitals do not conform to the standard, as with many intersex people, they are often nonconsensually mutilated to force them to fit one of the roles anyway.)

I emphasize the realness and the fact that there is beauty and power and lineage in *man* and *woman*, partly as a resource and validation for trans women and men but also as a reminder that our talk of gender being a construct does not invalidate its reality and importance to many people. As long as it is not something that is enforced on others, having a binary gender identity can be a healthy part of self-expression.

So what about nonbinary ancestry?

There are many examples, both modern and historical, of societies that already had nonbinary identities in them; a comprehensive list of them is outside the scope of this work for many reasons. Each of these had or has different roles and ways to express identities other than *man* or *woman* in their own culture.

Aside from all of the historical and modern cultures that boast more than two genders, within each and every culture there are people who the current gender system does not fit. I guarantee you, if a culture had a dozen genders and more than a dozen people, there would be people who do not fit within their gender paradigm. You can see them all through history. They are also a lineage, an ancestry, who look out for and support and are proud of their children.

Our sense of gender may come from innate feeling and understanding of ourselves, but it is shaped by the people who surround us and who come before us. We learn how to be a man or a woman by mimicking the men and women we see from an early age. Those who come before us are pivotal in how we embrace, embody, or reject gender.

EXERCISE: FINDING YOUR TRANS LINEAGE

I want you to think about the first trans person you met, whether or not they understood themselves as trans at the time that you met them. I want you to think about the first time you saw someone being themselves gender-wise and felt something inside you. Write a paragraph about them, how seeing them made you feel, and what you did as a result of that feeling.

I want you to think about everything you've read that has informed your gender and understanding of yourself in a healthy way. If you can, find out who wrote it (I know that can be hard on the internet, but it's still worth a shot). Write about how that affected you. Remember that the person who wrote it is also a person; consider what they said in light of what it says about who they are, and write something about them.

These people are your lineage. In a spiritual sense, if they are dead, they are your Ancestors, and thus potentially available for a healthy and reciprocal relationship. You are the living extension of a part of them, made manifest in the world. Knowing that, and knowing that each person you've written about was inspired by others and so on throughout history, how does that make you feel? Write about that.

EXERCISE: TRANS ANCESTOR WORK

Now that you've done that, try and incorporate the folks who have passed on from the previous exercise into your existing ancestor practice. Or, if you do not have one, set up a space with a neutral-colored cloth, a candle, some water for offering, and if you have any ideas of what they are, some offerings those from your trans lineage would like.

Spend a little bit of time there on a regular basis: every day if you can afford to, once a week if that's all you can do. Light the candle and talk to the dead, call them by name, let them know you have light and warmth and water and other offerings for them on your altar. Talk to them about how they inspired you and affected you. If you know songs that they liked, go ahead and sing them. If they had a spiritual practice that you are aware of, recite prayers or blessings from that tradition (where appropriate and within the bounds of your comfort); it can be a blessing for a living person to say prayers on behalf of the dead in many spiritual traditions.

Then listen. Spend time listening to them after honoring them and see if they have anything to say. If they make suggestions about offerings or objects they would like on your ancestor altar, pay heed to them (but remember it's okay to keep firm boundaries around what is possible and what is needed for you as well; this is a relationship). Talk to them about your life stuff, your problems, your complications, especially in areas where they have inspired you or otherwise specifically been your Ancestor. They may be able to help you in other ways; working with the dead is a human birthright and an essential part of many religious and spiritual paths.

EXERCISE: FINDING ANCESTORS OF GENDER

Whether you are cisgender, trans, or nonbinary, during the vast course of human history there are likely people who publicly or privately identified the way that you do. These are potential *Ancestors of Gender*, people who felt a similar way about themselves and embodied it in that way.

The above exercises focused on transgender lineage, but Ancestors of Gender exist regardless of whether you are trans or nonbinary. The process of finding them is similar, though.

If you are a man or a woman, you already have a leg up on this: you've seen other men or women in the past who have shaped how you present and express yourself. That's likely the case in your parents and many family members. Society is filled with people embracing, acting on, creating, and embodying these roles; it's not hard to find, because the gender binary is deeply encoded into the way we think, act, and speak.

If you are a man or a woman, when you describe yourself as that, who do you think of? When you talk about "good men" or "powerful women" or other positive role models of that gender, who do you think of? What qualities make those people admirable?

If there is a gendered style, accessory, type of clothing, etc. that you especially love and seek to emulate, who wore it that drew your attention to it?

Are there historical figures whose embodiment of their gender draws your attention? Do you style yourself after Boudica's ferocity or St. Francis's gentleness? Are you inspired by Olympias's fierce devotion to motherhood?

Remember, in this case these binary genders don't need to be limited. We aren't looking to narrow or define these categories; we are looking to find places to connect to them.

Also, trans men and trans women (and people who these days we might understand that way) are excellent Ancestors of Manhood and Womanhood. As with the above, they worked to expand those gender categories, and they worked to be themselves and embrace those identities, often in the face of resistance from society.

These are people who have and can inspire you. These are Ancestors who stood in the streams of people-who-understand-themselves-to-be-women, people-who-understand-themselves-to-be-men. These are Ancestors of Gender, of those specific genders, and powerful allies.

In this case, as in all cases with ancestor work, both collective ancestor veneration and hero worship are appropriate ways of interacting. If there is someone specific whose expression of gender moves you, they are a candidate for hero worship, but if you need a deeper and broader understanding of the many who have walked these paths before you, reach out to them collectively.

Journaling

Do you have any Ancestors whose gender presentation or expression stand out as particularly admirable to you? What is it about them that you relate to or admire?

Do you feel like you're in alignment with your Ancestors' understandings of your gender? Where do you align and where do you drift apart? Is there a component of how you express your gender that is based on parents or Ancestors? How do you feel about that?

FOUR
GODS AND GENDER

POLYTHEISM IS DEFINED BY belief in multiple gods, and modern Paganism by and large is influenced and derived from polytheistic belief systems. Different systems and cultures viewed their gods in different ways, but in most, the gods were seen as cosmic beings of great power and wisdom and connection, humanized in story but understood to be beyond humanity in scope. As cosmic beings, is gender something that is appropriate to be applied to them? As beings humanized in mythology, is there representation of trans and nonbinary identities in their stories? As modern worshippers, devotees, clergy, and enthusiasts, how do we see ourselves in and among the gods?

Trans Deities and Spirits

There are quite a few deities and spirits that trans folks look at and connect to on the basis of gender. In some cases (like those who are outwardly described as embodying multiple genders or reproductive roles) those connections may be obvious.

However, a good number of transgender people are binary and see themselves as men or women. For trans folks who center their identities in *man* and *woman* (even if there is a nonbinary element to their gender overall) deities whose gender is fluid, ambiguous, or otherwise more complex may not be resonant.

For a long time, I was told by Heathens and other worshippers of Germanic deities that I should be devoted to Loki because of their obvious fluidity. I railed against that; my thought was, "I'm a woman, not someone who is sometimes a man and sometimes a woman. What does Loki have to do with that?" The irony is that I both expanded my knowledge of my own gender and witnessed some fluidity (though for me it is between woman and agender, not woman and man). I also ended up becoming a devotee of Loki for completely different reasons but deeply honor him in all of her genderfluid, rebellious wildness.

This is a reminder, however, that trans experiences are not universal among us; we are all different in some way. For those who are centered in a binary identity of man or woman, deities who embody cultural connections to those qualities often come forward. Thus we have many trans women who have experiences of Freyja coming forward and guiding them in their transition, others with Aphrodite, Demeter, Persephone, and more. The point is, these deities come to people who need healthy representation, role models, and spiritual support in coming into themselves; while those deities may not be visibly nonbinary or trans in some way, they are still very helpful for people who wish to embrace that gender. Therefore, if you are *man* or *woman*, regardless of what else is in your story, it may be helpful to you to connect to deities that are firmly grounded in those concepts and identities.

Here is a list of Pagan deities who have some association with transgender people and identity, whether by ancient description or modern gnosis. This list is not exhaustive because it cannot be; trans and nonbinary folks find sacred representation and connection to our genders in all sorts of places. These are the deities I am the most aware of from personal practice and association as well as community interactions with other transgender Pagans and polytheists.

Freyja

Freyja is a Norse deity whose name means "Lady" in the sense of nobility. She is a deity well known for her beauty and magic and passion, and also her power in battle. She is one of the most commonly worshipped and honored deities among modern Pagans who are trans women and transfeminine. Freyja demands honesty to oneself; she expects greatness and expects people to embrace and embody their truth and power. While her legends do not necessarily point to a transfeminine nature, quite a few of her devotees have witnessed her that way. She wants us to see the beauty and power in ourselves, and bring it forward in a way that will stun the world.

Frey

Frey is Freyja's brother. Many modern trans men and trans-masculine people connect to Frey as a source of positive masculinity. He gives up his sword for love, though it costs him dearly. He is also a god called on primarily for peace, good seasons, prosperity, and good relations. In addition, his worship is often connected to the quotes of Saxo Grammaticus, who spoke of the Germanic priests dressing like women and being followed by the "unmanly clatter of the bells," something that appeals to transgender and nonbinary folks in many parts of the spectrum of gender.[5] Frey gladly embraces and protects those who approach him for support in these things.

Dionysos

I could write an entire chapter about Dionysos and gender; this many-faced, many-formed god of liberation, ecstasy, transformation, rebirth, and Mystery has always been viewed as queer in some way. One of the first times he came up in discussion was at a Pagan event I was attending that involved gender. People were discussing gender and gods, and one of his devotees spoke up and very firmly affirmed, "Dionysos is *not* a man."

One of his prominent epithets is Androgynos, or "Man-Woman" (yes, it comes from the same place as *androgynous*!). He has also been called the Womanly One. In Orphic beliefs, Dionysos is the third incarnation of Phanes, the all-gendered first-

---

5. Saxo Grammaticus, *The First Nine Books of the Danish History of Saxo Grammaticus*, trans. Oliver Elton, with additional material by Frederick York Powell (London: D. Nutt, 1894), 228.

born being who hatched from the cosmic egg at the beginning of time. People dressing as other genders, acting as other genders, and embracing their truest natures have always been a feature of his wild, ecstatic cults (where state religions have not tried to tame them).

As a god who has been reborn in many times and places, a god who has experienced all things, a shape-shifting god who can take on any form, and a god who wants humans to embrace their deepest natures and drives, Dionysos can support people going through difficult processes in transition. Those trying to change their skin to match their nature, trying to understand their own shifting natures, those suffering from madness and pain due to dysphoria, those ostracized by society for their choices, those who seek the power to be themselves in defiance of laws, customs, and the judgment of others—all can find solace in the Liberator.

Dionysos is the Liberator (*Eleutherios*) and the Loosener (*Lysios*). He can liberate people from the chains they place on themselves, as well as those others place on them. As Aristides said, "Nothing can be so firmly bound, by illness, by wrath, by fortune, or by anything else, that cannot be loosed by the lord Dionysos."[6] (This quote is also a fantastic invocation to liberate yourself and find freedom from things that bind you; chant it whenever you feel stuck or uncomfortable or bound, and pour out a little wine for him if you feel so inclined.) As the liberator, Dionysos wants you to be free in whatever ways are best for you, and he is absolutely appropriate to call on in relationship to wanting to be free to express and be your truest self.

---

6. I personally learned this quote through oral tradition, but it can be found in the *Orations* of Aelius Aristides, 4.29.

Kybele

Kybele (also spelled Cybele) is an ancient Anatolian goddess who was worshipped as Matar (Mother) by the Phrygian people. Images of a goddess by the same appearance were found in the same region, and based on archaeological evidence, her worship may date back as far as 6,000 BCE, long before written language that we recognize was used. Her worship became immensely popular and spread to Greece and Rome. She was known as the Mother of Gods and Men, the Phrygian Mother, and is called the Nurturer of All, All-Taming, lover of frenzy and ecstasy, and the Queen Whom the Drum Delights, among many other titles.[7] Kybele stands out because of her clergy and also because of a legend attached to her. Kybele's clergy included the Galli priests, people who were assigned male who would undergo castration and live as women and priestesses of her afterward, devoted to the Mother for life.

There is also a legend of how she (by the name of Agdistis in this legend) had both sets of genitals until she was tricked by the other gods into castrating herself, which sent her into a rage where she inflicted gender dysphoria on those surrounding her. While the legend is primarily a Hellenized version of a Phrygian story whose original has been lost to time, the essence remains clear: when you try to limit folks' gender (and when you try to mutilate intersex folks!) you are standing against Nature herself, and she is not going to be happy with you.

---

7. Apostolos N. Athanassakis and Benjamin M. Wolkow, trans., *The Orphic Hymns* (Baltimore, MD: John Hopkins University Press, 2013), 120.

In fact, the Mother doesn't mess around when it comes to her people. When the Roman Empire adopted the worship of Kybele (because a Sybil told them that her support was necessary to win the war on Carthage), they brought her Galli priestexes to Rome. Over time, the Roman state steadily Romanized the foreign cult, and this included preventing her clergy from castrating themselves. Eventually, the Galli priests were forced to stay in their temple compound rather than affront the dignity of the Romans with their feminine behavior and nature, only being allowed to leave once a year to beg for necessities to survive, and eventually the Roman state decided that the leadership of the Galli would be chosen by the state. While causation between the increasingly harsh treatment of the sacred trans clergy of the goddess that brought Rome victory and the decline of their empire can be left to the religious opinions of the individual, the correlation at the very least is rather damning.

The Mother loves transgender and nonbinary people and is a protector and champion of us. Even to this day I have encountered many trans women who have performed a dedication to her on the eve of their bottom surgeries, linking them to their ancient Ancestors and the mighty goddess they loved. Kybele will support you in listening to your deepest nature and self, the part of you that is who you are in the dark of the cave when nobody else is around. She will protect trans and nonbinary folks, sending her lions and other spirits as guardians. She can protect and guide you through surgery and other physical parts of transition. She can also connect you to the spirits of many Ancestors who observed similar circumstances and experiences to you. I will always recommend that trans and nonbinary people connect to Kybele for support and aid.

Loki

Loki is the first deity that many people think of when they think of any sort of gender fluidity or nonconformity. He's kind of a community icon the way Bugs Bunny is, and like Bugs Bunny, Loki is a prankster and trickster whose tricks are often turned on unjust authority (as in the *Lokasenna*) or against monsters (as in *Thrymskvitha* and the Faroese ballad *Loka Táttur*). Also like Bugs Bunny, her gender presentation changes as need suits: Loki was accused of having mothered many and been midwife to even more while on Midgard, they tricked the giant who was building Asgard's wall by turning into a mare and getting frisky with said giant's horse (also leading to the birth of Sleipnir), and served as Thor's handmaiden when Thor dressed as Freyja to retrieve his hammer from the giant Thrym.[8] Loki is chill; Loki is one of us (or we are of him; I've heard Heathens refer to trans people as Loki's kids).

In my experience, whether or not Loki is not only accepted but embraced by a Heathen group will give a good view into how they embrace trans people. I considered myself a Heathen for years, and someone I trust once told me, "Listen to how a Heathen group talks about Loki, and you will know how they feel about

---

8. *Lokasenna*, in *The Poetic Edda: Translated from the Icelandic with an Introduction and Notes*, Scandinavian Classics Volumes XXI and XXII, trans. Henry Adams Bellows (New York: The American Scandinavian Foundation, 1923), 159.

you." The Loki rule is a good rule of thumb; the groups I've been in where the attitude was "We nervously acknowledge that Loki is a god and will make propitiating statements about that once in a while" were likewise outwardly supportive of trans people but, at the end of the day, nervous and suspicious of us. On the other hand, where the attitude is closer to "Loki? Heck yeah!", those are far more likely to be the groups where trans folks are loved and celebrated.

Modern devotees of Loki are often trans, nonbinary, or in some way gender nonconforming. Loki sees us for who we are, witnesses how our societies wrongfully turn on us, knows how they try to bind us into shapes that please them and not ourselves, and has a fiercely protective love for trans and nonbinary people. She is also helpful to folks who have a naturally fluid quality to their gender or who are just generally unmoored in the concept of gender. She can help people who are trying to find ways to express and bring their gender out into visible and physical manifestation, i.e., shape-shifting. Finally, Loki loves sticking it to authority and is good to call on when said authority is being harmful and oppressive to trans folks; nobody likes pantsing the king like Loki does.

Odin

In the *Lokasenna*, it is mentioned that wherever Odin drinks, Loki drinks.[9] Some modern practitioners have taken that to mean that when you offer to one, you should offer to the other, and in light of me mentioning Loki, I feel like it's only appropriate to

---

9. *Lokasenna,*155.

mention Odin when talking about gods with interesting relationships to gender and trans folks.

In the same poem, Odin is mentioned as having been seen wearing women's clothes and practicing women's magic.[10] Magic —particularly *seidh*, a form of magic associated with both Odin and Freyja—was considered an unmanly practice. Practitioners were considered *ergi*, a word for a man who bottoms in a male-male pairing, which had associations with effeminacy and was a deadly insult at points in history.

Odin is a vast and powerful deity, the breath of the wind, the voice of ecstasy, madness, and poetry. He is not a god that one would imagine could be easily contained by the bounds of human gender. A trickster and shape-shifter himself, Odin takes on different forms and guises in his travels to fool others and to teach. Many modern practitioners whose gender is more fluid or simply hard to pin down connect to Odin as a deity who embodies how they approach and connect to gender.

Polytheism and Gender

I'm a polytheist and an animist. This work is created primarily for Pagans and Pagan-adjacent people in general. Many (though not all) Pagans are polytheist or use polytheist language as a framework for their practice.

Talking about the gods can be a touchy subject because everyone has different understandings and experiences of them. There are a lot of different ways to understand and approach them, even

---

10. *Lokasenna*, 160.

among members of the same traditions, much less a sprawling and poorly defined set of communities like "Paganism."

So before diving into gods and gender, I'm going to explain a little bit about my own theology so that you understand what I mean when I use certain terms. Understand that I know my framework may not work for everyone, and, as with anything in this book, you are free to approach things how you want. Especially in this section, I am not telling you what to believe, but what I've learned and experienced and what works in my practice.

I work with gods as relatively individual or collective beings who have their own wills, agendas, and spiritual identities. I think that sometimes two similar gods may be the same being, but deciding every god with a hammer is the same deity is like deciding that every person wearing flannel is the same person. I think it's generally respectful to treat them as individuals (except in cases where they are understood as collectives, such as the Norns, the Matronae, or really most deities that are referred to as plural in some way).

I understand gods as powerful spirits who carry particular types of energy, and often when we witness a representation or description of a deity that has a similar attribute, that attribute is representative of the greater power they wield. There are many Serpent gods, and they all carry the energy of the Serpent (regrowth, rebirth, transformation, traveling up and down the tree, life and death, poison and healing) as an example.

I understand gods as spirits who are in relationship with one another within the pantheons they are understood as being from, but as I also see them as living beings capable of change and growth, I also perceive their relationships with other deities changing and growing over time. I know many Vanic Bacchics, quite a few Christo-Pagans, folks who speak about the Morrigan working with Freyja and Odin, gnosis of Dionysos the liberator unbinding Loki from their imprisonment—modern beliefs based on spiritual experiences of groups of modern practitioners that seem to bear out over time and practice and interaction.

When I say *spirit*, I am generally referring to any being that exists who seems to possess a consciousness and yet is not embodied in the same way that we are, i.e., in what we understand as a living organic vessel. This broadly includes gods, formerly living humans (the Ancestors, the dead, etc.), what are considered spirits of nature or the world (nymphs, fauns, elementals, beings frequently called "fae," and many others), and less easily definable folks. It's a big category. Sometimes I sum things up as "gods, spirits, and the dead," meaning gods, former humans, and everybody else.

On the note of categorization, there are deified humans, incarnate gods, humans who become other kinds of spirits when they die (and other kinds of spirits who are born into human shape), and all sorts of cross-category examples. This isn't the *Dungeons and Dragons Monster Manual*; classifications are often vague or shift based on who is talking. As trans and nonbinary folks ourselves, we should understand that categories, when applied to others, are more for your own understanding than anything and that all sorts of beings defy easy categorization.

We are incarnate spirits; we are the spirits of our bodies, but also we are spirits that existed before our bodies and will exist after. We are conglomerations, collaborations, collectives; we are multitudes; we are legion—each single human being is. Where is the "I" in this? What are the parts that are of the body, and what are the parts that are of other places? We have hundreds or thousands of established systems of answers around those things, and those aren't questions I plan on answering for you here. But I do think that if you consider and practice the work in this book you will have a better overall understanding of how these concepts fit with you and work for you.

Spirits dance in and out of roles, changing, dying, transforming, and being reborn, sometimes in flesh, most often not. We don't currently have an objective, scientific way to express that, and that's okay for now. It is a framework and an understanding that for me and many others works to connect to sources of spiritual power and wisdom and guidance. It helps us to have influence over, and come to be in harmony with, ourselves and the world around us and our corner of the web of existence.

This is the framework I work with. That doesn't mean it's what I believe, though most of it comes from what I believe, which is based mostly off my own experience and the things I've witnessed checked against the wisdom of other humans living and dead. I think any person given to reflection about the world will change their opinion on -theism of any type, maybe even many times a day. Especially those of us who are deeply involved with spirit work, as it is not uncommon to have powerful experiences that are contradictory to common evidence or knowledge and yet still seem to bear weight in our lives.

There are many polytheist frameworks. Also popular is the polycentric model, which suggests that each deity is a whole and ultimate divinity in and of themselves, and as such has reflections of the other gods within their wholeness.[11] There are those who consider all deities to be ascended or advanced Ancestors, or who believe that the gods are agents of a greater deity, and more. The *poly* (meaning "many") in polytheism can carry a lot: there are many ways of looking at, understanding, and interacting with the many gods.

Belief in my framework isn't necessary to either read this book or benefit from the work it encourages. The essence of what I am saying is there regardless, and if it's something that calls to you, I trust you'll be able to find a way to adapt it to your own framework and cosmology and practice.

Anyway, let's get to gender and gods.

We are starting from the position that gender as we talk about it is primarily a human construct. That would mean deities (other than the ones who were pretty clearly elevated human Ancestors, and even then) have gender impressed upon them.

We are assigning gender to our gods. Someone beheld the spirit who brought healing and plague, who rode on the light of the sun and inspired humans to music and beauty, and said, "That's Apollon," and gendered him. Maybe it was their vision of that deity; maybe it was based on cultural assumptions, but someone, way back there, decided that they viewed this powerful being as a man, or as masculine.

As we've discussed, there are no specific categories that make someone a man or a woman, masculine or feminine, that are consistent across culture and time. So whatever qualities that Ances-

---

11. The polycentric model of polytheism is one that I've seen modern Neoplatonists discuss at length in the online community.

tor witnessed in relationship to Apollon that made them categorize them as male/man/masculine might have been interpreted differently through a different person, and we might consider Apollon a goddess, then.

I've spoken a bit about the ancestral connection with gender, and that bears examination and discussion as well. It may be tautological to say so, but the emphasis is important: if a culture gendered a deity a particular way, there is probably a cultural reason why that deity was seen in that way. The deity wasn't out there flashing physical genitals for people to make that determination. (And as we've discussed, in many premodern and Indigenous societies genitals weren't the be-all, end-all of gender that they are in our current colonized, unhealthy take.)

To some of these deities, that assigned gender might matter because of the relationship of the deity with the source culture that originally spoke about them. A spirit worker or polytheist who experiences direct gnostic interaction with deities should ask them specifically about that. There may be a reason it is valuable to interact with that deity that way.

That being said, a god is a powerful being with connections to humanity. If we move away from gendering-based-on-genitals and also move away from gendering-based-on-cultural attributes, what do we have left? Self-identification. Which moves the gendering of gods into the realms of the mystic and the gnostic, as there are few gods who speak up and say, "I am [man/woman/ what have you]."

I've encountered a great many people with direct interaction with deities and spirits who perceive them as a gender different than the cultural assignation handed down to us. Gods are bigger than humans, and even if they were once human, are not anymore. I don't know what gender is to the gods other than a way humans relate to them.

How would you relate to a deity you admire if they had been presented to you as having a different gender than the usual one they are shown with? How would you relate to a deity you were uncomfortable with if their gender was different? How would you relate to a deity that has no associations with trans people, who comes to you with a trans body?

I know so many trans women who worship Freyja, and she forced them to confront the truth about their identity. (I am one of them; I would not have come out if she hadn't pushed me.) Not a few of us witness her as transfeminine. I know many trans men who worship Freyr as a shining example of nontoxic masculinity and who witness him as transmasculine. I've known people who worship the Dagda and Dionysos as trans men and who witness Kybele and Ariadne as trans women. I know so many people who disregard gender entirely when it comes to deities.

My point is this: unless a god tells you that how you view their gender is important to them (and, honestly, I've had deities do this with me, especially in relation to how I relate to them), why are you giving them a particular one? Again, gender is a form of categorization; what attributes are you categorizing them by? Are there others that might cause you to see them differently? Is there a reason other than tradition that you assign a particular gender to a particular deity? It's fine to gender them whatever way you please, but ask yourself why you are doing that.

EXERCISE: TRANSING THE GODS

This exercise is primarily for trans and nonbinary folks. I encourage cis folks to read through it, think about it, and also keep in mind that you do not understand the experience of being trans.

Trans folks sometimes talk about "transing" a character, which means finding representation in a character who is not explicitly presented as transgender. There is a serious lack of transgender characters written by transgender people in media and literature, so naturally, when we want to see ourselves in a story, we find the people who have some experiences in common with us.

An idea circulating online for transing characters can be summed up this way: every character is trans unless specifically noted as cisgender. This rule neatly turns cissexism on its head, and it also reminds us that our experience is a human one and one that can be found in many places.

If you look through trans spaces online and talk to trans folks in person, we will often have characters we have decided are transgender either individually or collectively. It's also interesting that most cisgender people, when they hear about transing a character, think of making the character a different gender, rather than finding the relatable struggles of a character who isn't specifically noted as transgender.

I definitely believe there is a gulf of difference between pop culture figures and a god with an established relationship with humanity and ability to affect the world, though I will agree that there are places where those lines blur, and often those places are where spirits and deities choose to show themselves differently to different people (or are perceived differently by different people).

That leads us back to the point: we perceive these beings differently, but if our relationships with them are still (or more) mutually beneficial as a result, the differences are beneficial as well.

That being said, part of devotion is coming to understand a deity better, and people often gravitate to the powers they find the most relatable. If you can understand and relate to a deity on a deeper level because of who you are, then that is a powerful thing.

Trans folks: what part of your experience of being transgender or nonbinary matches your understanding of something that a deity went through? Where would it make sense for a deity or spirit you revere to have a trans identity? I'm going to share a few examples with you.

A version of the story of Dionysos has him dressing in girl's clothing until he grew up and could protect himself. I know transmasculine folks who identify with that story, given that many of them were also forced to dress and act as girls until they came to the place in life where they could stand up for themselves.

Loki changes their body and apparent gender to match the needs of the situation. They turned into a mare to seduce a horse, and Odin accused them of mothering and being midwife to many children on Midgard (and, it is worth mentioning, Loki snarked that Odin was one to talk, since he had dressed in women's clothes to learn women's magic).[12] It's no surprise that many genderfluid folks see reflections of themselves in Loki and Odin.

As noted before, Kybele also had a trans priesthood; it is unsurprising that many trans women identify with and connect to Kybele.

---

12. *Lokasenna*, 159–60.

It doesn't even need to specifically be about perceived gender and transition in the story, either. I know many bold, powerful, beautiful trans women who connect to Freyja because they share magic, beauty, strength in adversity, sexuality, and love of bright and shiny things with her. I've seen transmasculine folks talk about seeing themselves in the healthy masculinity of the Dagda or Yngvi Frey.

You don't even need a reason. If you feel it and examine why you feel it, you may come to understand it, and I encourage you to follow that feeling if you have it. Doing that has opened a lot of doors to connection with my own holy powers.

Being cisgender is not the default of humanity; humanity comes in a wildly diverse rainbow, and identifying with the gender assigned to you at birth based on the outward appearance of your genitals is only one of many ways to be human. The gods only have the genders we assigned to them because they were ways for people to understand them. If you understand them differently because you understand gender differently, there is nothing wrong with you; in fact, that is a deeply human and sacred experience that is yours and between you and that being.

Journaling

Who are the gods closest to you or who draw your attention the most? How do the representations of them express the gender assigned to them in mythology? How would seeing them as beyond human considerations of gender affect your relationship with and understanding of them? How would seeing them manifest as another gender affect your understanding of them?

FIVE
WHO ARE YOU?

WE'RE HERE TALKING ABOUT gender and the self (with an eye toward creating spiritual wholeness), and it seems that we may need a bit more definition on what the *self* is. I'm not going to try and challenge or counter claims others have made about this. Philosophy, religion, and science have been finding different ways to answer this question for as long as we've been able to ask it.

However, when we think of our "self" we usually think of one particular thing, bounded by our bodies, and those are assumptions that we will need to untether from a bit if we want to move forward effectively in this discussion.

Souls

What's a soul?

In modern Western Christianity there is the idea of a single soul, a single spiritual self, that inhabits the body and goes through changes after death. Despite the protestations of many, this is not a unique idea; the concept of a "sole soul" is a fairly widespread one in different faiths and belief systems, and I am absolutely not here to discount it.

There are models of multiple souls—different energetic bodies, beings, parts, identities—that make up a whole. Many of the systems that include multiple souls (such as the Kemetic and Heathen multipart souls) include the physical body among the souls.

Regardless, cultures that engage in animist and polytheist practice generally have a concept of part of a human that survives death. The ultimate fate of that part is up for debate depending on the system; in some cases people rejoin the Ancestors, in some cases they are reborn, in some cases they become another kind of being. In fact, most cultures without a monolithic religion (and even some that do) have debates about "what happens," because in stories, a lot of different things happen, even in a single culture. (And it's worth noting that the things we think of as Greek, Germanic, etc. culture are a reductionist attempt to boil down the ideas and practices of diverse groups of people over hundreds or thousands of years, and thus, doomed to failure.)

But regardless of post-life fate, the idea of an eternal part of you is central to this work. We aren't going to answer too many of the nitty-gritty questions about this, partly because I want this work to be accessible to people of relatively diverse belief frame-works, but also because my experience has led me to believe that you really need to work that out on your own with the experiences you have in life with the dead.

Many trans and nonbinary folks feel their gender on a level that is spiritual as well, and that can manifest in many different ways. Some trans folks unpack their gender and gender-based needs as being a manifestation of being born into the "wrong" body. That definitely isn't the best framing for everyone, but being born into a body that does not match your felt sense of self is absolutely challenging, and those experiences are absolutely valid as well. If this is a narrative that rings true to you, it's likely that you feel there is a spiritual element to your transness; being born into a body that challenges your identity suggests that your identity may not come wholly from your body and that it may have existed pre-birth.

If being challenged by the shape of the body given to you at birth is a narrative that you embrace, consider where the original feeling comes from. Is it from another physical incarnation that you experienced prior to this one? Is it part of a powerful ancestral current that you feel manifests deeply in some part of your non-physical self? For those who feel harmed by this (as someone who experiences some of my body dysphoria in a similar way, I have struggled with this much of my life), this can be difficult work; it may be worth spending time in meditation with your holy powers asking them *why*. Sometimes they can provide context that helps to settle your feelings about it, and regardless, they can often pro-vide suggestions on ways to deal with it and empower yourself in relationship to this challenge.

Body

We know our bodies because they are physically manifest, visible, tangible things. They are part of us, and being embodied is the common experience shared by everyone who is reading this (as far as I know!).

It's not a far cry to say that our bodies are part of us, even when it doesn't feel that way. We've discussed gender dysphoria and the body dysphoria that often accompanies it; many trans folks have a narrative or understanding of being born in the "wrong" bodies or their bodies not developing the way they should have in utero, during puberty, and so on. While there are those who would decry this narrative, it's common enough among transgender people, though it is important to recognize that it is far from the only narrative.

One of the goals of people who undergo medical transition is to see their outsides match their insides—see their body match how they perceive their mind, their soul, their essence. I consider this to be one of the holiest and most powerful journeys that one can undertake; within each of us is a spark of divinity, a Starry nature that longs to be manifest. Trans folks who manage to bring forward the hidden parts of themselves often have remarkably positive life changes as a result, and not all of them stem from the psychological impact of no longer having that dichotomy between soul and body. This alchemy is a great work; we are given imperfect bodies that do not reflect our natures, but as we work to help them reflect our natures more, more of our own selves and power manifest.

I feel that this also extends far beyond sculpting and remaking your body to fit socially accepted gender, though. I have known people who experimented with all sorts of body modifications to bring their true self forward, often in ways that didn't seem to line up with specific gendered expectations. That is no less a sacred journey.

Anyway, in English we speak of body "parts," from different organs like your heart and lungs and brain, to different regions with functions, like hands and feet and head. Each of those parts can be discrete in some ways but connected in others; where we draw those lines is often (but not always) arbitrary, just as the lines we draw with gender.

EXERCISE: WHERE DO YOU BEGIN AND END?

Where does your body begin and end, though? We like to think that the skin is the boundary of our bodies, but in fact it is a permeable region, designed to allow in certain things and expel certain things. There are few tissues in our body that are not, in some way, permeable; our biology would not function very well otherwise.

I want you to consider other things such as breath. When you breathe, you exhale matter that has been touched by you—air molecules that have been changed as they traveled through your body, water vapor that has been processed by you, many thousands of microscopic organisms in each breath that may have spent time living in you, eating what you eat, breathing what you breathe. Where you breathe, you leave parts of yourself.

Consider your waste—your urine, feces, sweat, and other substances that you exude to take harmful things outside of your body. All of those things are full of your DNA, of the things that have been part of your body.

Think about your body heat. Think of the energy that radiates out from you. There are many energies, both those quantified by science and those that so far have only been witnessed experientially, that emanate from your form. Those energies are part of you, and they change the world around you. They are shaped by you: by your activity, your food, your drink, and the very shape of your body. You are constantly emanating waves of energy.

Think about your words and the things that you say. Think of how the things that you say and do affect the world around you on an immediate level, and all the ways that they cascade out into reality. Each of those words has found an origin in your unique situation, your wholeness of mind, body, soul, and any other parts you care to name. These words were affected by your sleep patterns, your gut bacteria, your childhood upbringing, the weather—all these things that affect your body.

Think about your clothing. Think about how what you wear is shaped by you, just as your body is shaped by it. These fibers that sit on you, that frame you and protect you from the elements, are also things that you wear to express yourself (if you have the privilege to have any choice in your clothing). Think about how deeply your clothing can affect how you feel and function: a pair of shoes with a hole in them, a coat with a tear, sweatpants with a busted drawstring, or underwear that slides down your ass—how do these things affect you?

Think about your friends and family and loved ones. Think about the people who have most directly breathed your air, shared your saliva through food and drink or kisses, sweat through shared activity, sexual juices through shared physical intimacy, thoughts through shared conversation, sacred energies through shared rites. Think of the ways that all of these things have affected them and affected you.

Where does your body begin and end? Where do you begin and end? Having considered all of this, who are you?

Clothing Is Part of Your Body Too

Clothing (and makeup, jewelry, and accessories, including our technology and other things that we carry with us all the time) contain social signals. Some of those social signals are what some folks call *gender cues*. Gender cues are the signals that tell someone how to categorize someone else based on their gender. We make split-second decisions about what someone's gender is, usually without thought, partly because there is so much social coding around gender and appearance.

A genderfluid acquaintance of mine used to say that having six gender cues of one sort or another was usually enough to get the idea across. While I think that varies based both on the viewer and the cue-er, I think it's a good guideline for how this kind of stuff works. Most of those cues that they were describing are things that are added or subtracted to your appearance but not really considered part of your body; a lot of them involve clothing and the way it sits on you, makeup and facial hair or lack thereof, the way you wear your hair, etc. There are a lot of potential ways for these things to manifest and be changed around. Of course, not every cue is something that's available to everyone.

The thing is, we internalize these gender cues as well. When we look in the mirror and don't see the person we want to see, it can be because some of those things are missing.

Time to tell another personal story.

Originally, when I had planned to come out as transgender, I spent a good deal of time in consideration of how I wanted to dress and what I wanted to wear. I had a deep argument with myself, which went something like this:

"The purpose of clothing is environmental protection. No clothing inherently belongs to one gender or another. Therefore, after I come out, I do not need to change my style of clothing at all."

It didn't work out that way, but it took me years to understand the many reasons why. A lot of it has been struggling with internalized misogyny and also social anxiety. I eventually started changing the way I dressed after I started to broaden and deepen my understanding of gender and also recognized that just because I didn't know *why* something was helpful didn't mean that it wasn't.

I spent years trying to dress androgynously because I felt that it was important to deconstruct harmful ideas about gendered clothing, and because I did not want to give in to those ideas. The result: I felt righteous about my choices but ultimately miserable.

A friend was getting rid of more feminine clothing in a "tran-me-down" (when trans people exchange clothing that no longer fits their gender expression), and trying it on, I felt right and good and powerful. Looking in the mirror, I felt euphoria about my appearance that I hadn't often felt before in my life. I started to recognize that clothing *did* matter to me, that feminine-coded things were things that were appealing to me, and that all of this mattered and was important. I like dresses; I like nail polish. I acknowledge that these things are only coded as feminine socially, and I like them partly because of that, and partly because they feel right to me. A man, trans or cis, who likewise likes those things is no less a man for it; nor am I any less of a woman (or nonbinary, or a feminist) for enjoying them.

Why does it matter? Because clothing is part of your self. It hangs on your body and reflects, based on social values and other things, who you are. When it doesn't reflect who you are, it's often uncomfortable and unpleasant. When it does, it's often pleasing and euphoric. Something as simple as a shift in color or cut can change how you feel about yourself entirely. It's okay to acknowledge that, trust me; it doesn't make you shallow or a traitor to "good gender theory" to acknowledge that some clothing (and accessories, etc.) help to reflect what you feel on the inside. It's valid to question why that is, and if you don't like the reasons you find, to work on the assumptions around those reasons.

But at the end of the day, the point of the exercise here is to manifest your self in all the ways that you can so that divine voice within you can speak to you and through you with the greatest clarity possible. I ask you again, who are you? Now I ask: What choices do you make involving your clothing that reinforce that? What changes would you make to how you dress given the opportunity? Is there a way to make those changes? What have you got to lose?

EXERCISE: WHAT STYLES HAVE MADE ME HAPPY?

For this exercise, all you need is the ability to write and record your thoughts. Things that might be helpful, though, include old photos of you, as well as images of people or beings that you admire.

First, I'd like you to think about old styles you've embraced. If you have them available and it's something that you can do, look over old images of you. When you see or remember a particular hairstyle or piece of clothing that made you happy, note it and write it down. Once you have written it down, ask yourself if you know why it made you feel that way. Write that down too.

Now consider the styles of the people or beings that you admire. What particular things stand out to you? Is it a part of their look, how they carry themselves, how they speak? Is it a particular thing that they do? All of these things are important. Run them through the same question as you did with personal attributes: why does this attribute make me feel this way? Then ask yourself, how would I feel if this was an attribute that was part of me? How would I feel in this outfit, with this hair, making this gesture, carrying myself this way, speaking this way, etc.?

Something I am going to emphasize again here: *why* is important, but it is the hardest question to answer. If you don't know *why* something makes you feel that way, consider it a bit but leave it blank. We are in the process of exploring the whats and the whys, and you don't need to have all the answers right away.

Community

The saying goes, "A man is known for the company he keeps." This applies to women and nonbinary people as well. It's hard to separate a person from the people they choose to associate with.

Who do you choose to surround yourself with? Who do you call or message when you're having a bad day? What about when something wonderful happens? Who are the people you connect to regularly?

Think back to the "Where Do You Begin and End?" exercise and what you considered there. Remember all the ways that we not only affect the world around us but are part of that world. The people who you talk to, even if they don't see you in person, are affected by the minutiae of your life in the reasons that you contact them, the way that you contact them, what you say or express to them, and how you leave them feeling.

When we get to the people we interact with in-person, the effect of ourselves becomes even greater. We warm one another with our body heat and share air and microorganisms as we breathe and talk and laugh and sing together. We shed parts of our skin that become dust and are inhaled or swallowed by those we are around. We share moods, we synchronize some of our hormonal cycles, and shared meals lead to the same foods being in separate bodies.

We share the physical, the emotional, the spiritual, the energetic aspects of ourselves with the people around us. We shape the people around us just by being alive, and shape them more the more we spend time with them. In some ways, saying that you like being around someone is saying that you like the shape that them being in your life gives you: "I like how you shape me." This effect goes the other way as well: who you are, what you do, what you take in and put out affects those around you.

So part of you is your community. For me, I like to think of community as people who assemble for shared purposes and thus end up building connections. The earliest human communities were likely extended families who settled into one geographic region or followed one particular kind of herd animal, banding together for survival. When humans are small groups of hunters and gatherers across the face of the world, it's hard to really know people from other families. We sat around the fire together at night, looked at the stars above us, watched as the sparks of our shared heart drifted up toward them, and told great stories and dreamed great dreams. Those first human communities have had unknown and mighty impact on who we've become. Think of how the communities that you are a part of may affect others in the future as well.

Over time, humans became plentiful enough that they banded together over other things. Shared resources in geographic locations, shared religion, shared ideals, shared lineages. In these busy and noisy times, there are so many ways that we overlap and interact with one another: we have shared crafting groups, groups formed around political action and social transformation, shared identity and sexuality, and more. All of these interlocking communities, from the people you share meals with to the people you chat with online to the people you work with and the people you pray with, all of these are part of your community.

If you think of community being around a hearth and think of a fire within yourself, you can ask yourself, who comes to warm themselves at my fire? Who shares the fire that is me? Who does it by choice and who does it by necessity? How does that shape me?

How does this relate to gender, then?

We've discussed how gender presentation is socially determined by a combination of visual cues, social behaviors, clothing, etc., and how different societies have vastly different ideas of gender. Each community that you are in some way a part of, whether by choice or not, has their own ideas about gender, and as we all know, those ideas about gender tend to be socially enforced too.

Trans folks are familiar with this and how it works. If your family (a community) has rules around gender that say, for instance, if you are assigned male at birth then you will always be male, and you are assigned male at birth and are definitely *not* male, you know that you are going to be deeply affected by your community because they don't recognize your gender. This varies from community to community as well, so a single person can be treated as and perceived as different genders by different communities that they are a part of: family could support who they are while their workplace rejects it, their religious groups accept it conditionally, and their arts and crafts groups don't care, for example.

The ideas around those norms affect the way we are. Most of the time those acceptances and unspoken agreements around gender are not 100 percent impermeable; most people will accept some level of gender variance while still denying a trans person the whole of their identity. So for the example of the trans woman whose family doesn't accept them as anything but a man, this might change over time as they present and perform in ways that are considered "normal" for a woman, and over time their family may acknowledge their womanhood in limited contexts: taking the role of a bridesmaid because it would look foolish for her to dress like a man, being more comfortable with her being with male partners because that's what a woman "should" do (thank you, heterosexism!).

Cisgender people are absolutely affected by this as well. Women are routinely mocked for having "masculine" features or interests, men are harassed and abused for not being "manly" enough (it's almost like society places a certain value on "man" and "male" things), and many other examples besides. This kind of selective acceptance of a person's gender is toxic and causes lots of harm, but that's not the whole of the subject at hand.

The fact is, the girl who gets called "one of the boys," the boy who gets mocked and called a sissy or a girl for not liking football, the nonbinary people of all stripes, they all experience their inter-action with gender differently depending on the social group that they are a part of. Their core sense of self, I believe, remains intact, but on top of that core are layer after layer of social obligations—a Sargasso Sea of gender rules, regulations, and guidelines enforced by the norms of their varying social groups. How many people call themselves into question because of the way that their own gender expression is treated? Most of us do.

Many trans people are forced to make compromises. "I can only be a woman in private at home, or my wife will leave me and take the kids." "I can't tell anyone I'm a boy; I'm afraid of what people will try to do to me to 'prove' that I'm a woman." "I don't bother with my name and pronouns with those people; when I try to, they just call me 'it.'" I wish all those examples were fictional or hyperbole, rather than things I hear daily from my trans and non-binary kin. The effect that social enforcement of gender has on us is huge and frequently devastating, and I, for one, want to work toward a world where that is no longer an issue.

So while our core self and how we categorize it—our sacred gender—may not change based on the observations of and interactions with others, so many of our pieces of gender expression and social gender identity shift because of who we are around.

Needless to say, I strongly encourage people to stick with those who will accept them when they have the choice. The sacred star of yourself, that hearth fire within you, is nurtured by being around those who will accept that you are who you say that you are, who know that you know the truest nature of yourself better than anyone else can.

We are all forced in one way or another to interact with and be part of communities that aren't supportive of who we are in some way. There are a lot of potential strategies for dealing with that; it's very situational and based on a lot of different factors.

I'll tell you how I survived it, and I hear and see similar stories from other trans folks all the time. For the better part of my life, I pretended to be a boy or a man. I was terrible at it, but I did my best to pretend to protect myself; for a long time, I lived in places where being myself was simply not an option. I did the small and private things to affirm to myself that I was a woman. I would polish my toenails because people couldn't see them except at home (and even then, only if I took off my socks, which in a cold climate is often optional). I would wear women's underwear. I would find women's clothing that looked like men's clothing to the point where unless someone was looking very closely and carefully, they would not know. (Men never did; women rarely did, and when they did it was usually accompanied by some kind of compliment.) I listened to female singer-songwriters who spoke to me as a woman. I played video games with female characters, read woman authors and fiction where the main characters were women. I worshipped goddesses known for their connection to things that our society (or that I personally) associated with being a woman.

I had daily affirmations. "I'm basically a woman." "No one knows, but I'm a woman." I came to feel a strength and pride in it. The men who surrounded me who said horrible things about women didn't know that there was a spy in their midst; the women who would comment on me getting along so well with other women and being "chicky" at times didn't know that they had a secret sister trying to lift them up.

Within me was a truth that no one could take away from me, a fire so deep and safe, tended carefully by me over time, a fire that warmed the parts of me that no one else warmed, that no one could take away from me. Despite what others would consider evidence to the contrary, despite misunderstandings and misinterpretations of my actions and behavior, despite the crushing weight of patriarchal, cissexist society: I knew that I was a woman. I knew that *woman* was hard to define, but I knew that it was an important part of me at the core. That fire was something no one could ever take from me. That star inside me blazed quietly, until I found healthy community that I could show it to and share it with, which led to me nurturing it and raising it up so that I could share it with the world, bring the inside out, and live as the person I knew myself to be.

EXERCISE: SPIRITS OF YOUR COMMUNITIES

Every community or group has spirits or deities who are associated with it, whether formally and by choice or casually by association and just existing.

More so, many believe that there are specific spirits *of* organizations and communities that can be approached. Some believe that they are *egregores*, spirits created by collective intent and imagination. Others witness them as spirits sent by deities or ancestral groups to foster, support, and take on a central role in the health and well-being of the group. Both may be simultaneously correct.

When you are transitioning socially, or considering doing so, even if it is as small a change as asking people to use a different pronoun set, it can be helpful to connect to the spirits of the groups that you are a part of to ask for support for and ease in those changes. This can also be a useful exercise if you are experiencing difficulty with the social aspects of your transition in relationship to members of that group. If folks in the group are giving you trouble, take it to the spirits of the group; it's their problem too.

A simple way to do that is to use the symbol of the group as a focus. Prepare a neutral space (it can be as simple as setting down a cloth to indicate a separate space), and put a symbol or symbols associated with that group in the space. Do not put down symbols associated with individual people; you aren't looking to talk to their spirits but rather the spirits of the group as a whole.

Do some cleansing of yourself and the space and light a candle. Look on the symbols and breathe. Think about the best values of that group, the parts of its spirit that you connect to, identify with, and embrace. If there are deities associated with the group, you may want to open with prayers to them and ask them to help support and guide this process.

Speak the name of the group three times. Then call to the spirits that oversee the group. You can say something like,

> *Spirits who guide and support [X group or community], I call to you.*
>
> *Spirits who embody the values of [XYZ] for [X community], I call to you.*
>
> *Spirits who guide the greater destiny of [X community], I call to you.*
>
> *Spirits who support the well-being of [X community] and its members, I call to you.*
>
> *Spirits of [X community], I call to you.*

You can repeat this invocation three times or until you feel heard.

Address the spirits respectfully; if you can provide an offering in the form of incense, water, or something appropriate to the community in question, then this is a good time for it. Explain the situation, explain the changes that you want to make and your concerns about how people will deal with them, or explain the trouble that you are having in your transition.

Remind the spirits you have called on that they are responsible for the health and functioning of the group, and that the group dynamic has to be healthy for the community to be healthy. Emphasize that you want to be treated with dignity and be seen as you are, and that the health of the group relies on the individual sovereignty of its members being recognized within the group. Ask for what help or support you need.

Take some time to listen. If you get impressions, write them down. It's also a good time to divine. Using a divination method of your choice that feels appropriate, ask the spirits for their response, what might be able to help them help you and thus help the group.

You may run into groups whose spirits are unwilling to work with you at all on this, and if that seems to be the case and is reflected in the behavior of the embodied community members, then it should be clear that the group is either not for you or you will have to take on a lot of responsibility and labor to change the group to fit you. Sometimes it's good to stay and fight, and sometimes we have the strength, energy, and social and emotional support for it. Sometimes it's time to move on, and if you don't feel like you can reach an understanding with the spirits and living people in the group, it may be time to face that. In that case, it is appropriate to thank the spirits and ask them for safe and healthy closure for yourself as you move on to better pastures.

Ancestors

If your living community is part of you and you are part of it, certainly your Ancestors are as well in many of the same ways.

Consider all of the factors that led to your entanglements with gender. The people who raised you learned about gender from their parents and the societies that they were raised in. Those teachings about gender from Ancestors of blood and familial lineage are often key to shaping early perceptions of the self in relationship to the world.

So, too, do thinkers about gender, for good or ill, affect our understanding of it. Religious leaders, philosophers, authors, writers, poets, artists all have had different things to say about it at different points.

As we've discussed in the chapter about Ancestors, all of these people have shaped who you are. Your lineages are part of you, and you are part of them. You are the living embodiment of those who have come before (among many other things), guided and shaped by them, and they affect the world still through you. By doing well, you credit and support the Ancestors that support you.

In a very real way, we are our Ancestors. Consider the ways that your dead and Ancestors may affect your perceptions and understandings of yourself and your gender as well.

Drawing It Together

So what can you take away from all this talk of "Where do I begin and end"?

1. We are all, in many ways, composite beings, affected and shaped by the things and people around us.

2. Nevertheless, there are core parts of us that are uniquely us, that are nurtured or weakened by how we manifest them in body, in spirit, and in community.

3. To strengthen and manifest those core parts of yourself, it is important to bring body and presentation into harmony with them, and to find social community that harmonizes with your understanding of yourself too.

Journaling

Who are you in the world and in relationship to other people? How do they see your gender? Are you happy or content with how you are perceived? If not, what could be missing? Are you content with how people treat you in relationship to your sense of identity? If not, what would be ideal for you?

SIX
ELEMENTS OF GENDER

AN *ELEMENT* IS A piece or part of something, a basic building block of what makes something up. Everything can be reduced to smaller parts as far as we've been able to find, and conceptually looking at individual elements that make something up can provide us with an understanding of what they really are. When a whole picture is fuzzy or uncertain, breaking it down can help us find those parts that make it up and where they fit together.

Gender Euphoria: The Smile Test

Remember when we talked about gender dysphoria versus gender euphoria? We're going to talk about the Smile Test.[13] The Smile Test is a simple one, and one of the best ways to help figure out what gendered things work best and are most affirming to you. It would come from folks coming to our meetings and freezing up when we got to asking them their pronouns. "Oh … whatever you want to use," was a frequent answer.

Now, being fair, there are plenty of people who are very comfortable with "Whatever you want to use." However, if you're a trans person being brave and coming out to a group that you've never been around before, or if you're shy and are used to being given a hard time about your gender identity, you might want to soft-peddle things a bit, and "Whatever you want to use" is a frequent way of soft-peddling and pulling back to protect yourself. If you're putting yourself out on a limb and are in a circumstance where people may use pronouns other than the ones that you were assigned for the very first time, there's a good chance that you may want that to happen. But how to ask that?

We would always ask, "Well, which pronouns make you smile?" and then go through a list of them. Frequently, shyly, someone would ask for a particular set, and seeing the way that their faces lit up when those pronouns were used consistently over the course of the night by a room full of strangers was a beautiful sight to behold.

---

13. A concept introduced to me by Maur DeLaney of Genesee Valley Gender Variants, a Rochester-based trans and nonbinary meetup group that has been running for many years, and which I have had the pleasure of attending for a few of those years.

The Smile Test applies to a lot of other things, and one of the things it most consistently applies to is gender and figuring out what things bring you gender euphoria. It can be a hard journey—at the beginning I was resistant and often worded it as, "Well, nothing makes me smile, but this makes me grimace less." But a lot of that was a function of not being willing to dare to embrace the things that genuinely would make me smile (and some of it was not knowing that they existed or what they were).

It can be complicated, too, trying to figure out what fits you when so many of the things are things that you haven't tried on before, either literally or metaphorically. You have to start somewhere, though, if you want to find yourself.

So what makes you smile? Are there clothes you see other people wearing that you feel a pang about, worrying whether they would look good on you or not, but, regardless, you feel them touch something deep inside? Clothes are one of the first places to look for sources of gender euphoria, as they are one of the primary markers of gender in our culture. Don't worry with an individual item or even with a whole look about them being "masculine" or "feminine" clothes; those are externally applied criteria that have nothing to do with your perception of them. Do they make you feel good? Does the idea of wearing them make you smile? Then they are clothes for your gender, regardless of what your gender is.

What about names? Trans and nonbinary folks often change our names to reflect our changing understanding of ourselves, coupled with how we would like to be perceived. Are there names that you keep going back to, names of characters in fiction or historical figures that tug at you when you read them? If you play video or roleplaying games, are there names that you tend to use for the characters in those (especially if those characters don't match your birth-assigned gender)? Imagine someone calling you one of those names—does it make you smile?

Pronouns! There are so many of them! One of the things that pronouns do is put you into a category with other people socially, and that's one of the many reasons that they are so important; *he* lumps you in with men, generally, and *she* with women. *They* could associate you with nonbinary folks in general. There is also an always-expanding list of neopronouns that you can play with too, or create your own! (Neopronouns are groups outside of the standard English he/him, she/her, and they/their, often used to represent nonbinary identities; popular examples include fae/faer, zie/zir, sie/hir, and e/em/er, though there are new ones all the time.) Remember, gender and pronouns are not always linked; *he* doesn't have to be masculine and *she* doesn't have to be feminine. Pronouns are like little names, the names we use for people and things when we don't want to repeat their full name over and over in a sentence; what little names make you smile? I want you to imagine people calling you different pronouns and see which set or sets make you smile when you imagine it.

What about accessories? Jewelry, makeup, bags, belts, things you carry on your person or keep around you that aren't necessarily for covering your nakedness? Jewelry and makeup are both frequently involved with gender coding in modern Western culture, and both are generally considered feminine, though there are "acceptable" forms of either for masculine presentation as well. We aren't terribly worried about "acceptable" though, and even though I'm primarily interested in other women and nonbinary folks, I can admit the aesthetic appeal of a guy wearing guyliner. What accessories, flair, baubles, and doodads make you smile? Think of things you've seen other people wear, things you've seen on Etsy or on the shelves of brick-and-mortar stores, things that you wished in some small way that you had. Imagine yourself wearing them, and perhaps, most importantly, imagine other people complimenting you on them. Which ones make you smile?

You get the idea. Each of those things are things that apply directly to your person: names, clothes, and accessories are things that surround you, specifically. We can expand this, though, because as we discuss in "Clothing Is Part of Your Body Too," your personal physical self is not the boundary of yourself, just one particular locus of it. What about your home and decorations? Your furniture, your carpets, your books, your food? Seriously, think about those things in relationship with yourself. Think about those things and see if they make you smile. And if they don't make you smile, I'd like you to consider other options for things in the same category (including just not having whatever it happens to be) and see which of those options brings a smile to your face.

This can be expanded as well. I'd like you to think about the people you spend your time around, the activities that you choose to take part in, the jobs that you end up in. I want you to go through each of those things, any of the things in your life that you have any amount of choice in (and yes, you have choice of name and identity; you have more choice over most of these things than you've been trained to think you do), and put them through the Smile Test, and keep testing alternatives until one makes you smile.

This is some of the deepest and most powerful trans magic. It may sound silly to you, but it reflects a deep reality: your body has a wisdom that your mind has trouble accessing consciously. The things that make us smile often break through our thoughts and mental considerations, and a smile dawns on our face like the rising sun, bringing light, knowledge, and certainty: *This thing is good. This thing is good for me.*

The Smile Test is a deep and powerful somatic magic, something that resonates with the deeper parts of yourself, and one that can help you to find the things that are aligned with you.

I want you to list each of the things from each of these categories mentioned above that made you smile when you imagined them applied to you: names, pronouns, clothes, accessories, living space.

For the ones that involve how people interact with you (names and pronouns especially), I want you to ask one person in your life to try using those things with you. It doesn't have to be publicly (though it can be); it can just be in private conversations between the two of you.

How does it feel when you hear those names? How does it feel when you hear yourself being called by those pronouns? Do you smile? Do you feel awkward, as though you don't deserve them? That's impostor syndrome, and we all get it. Push past that feeling, and remember, go for the smile.

For things such as clothing and living quarters, I'd like you to take one thing from each of those lists and try them out as well. Try and wear them around people who are genuine with you and who care about you. We don't need brutal honesty (which, to be fair, is usually more about brutality than honesty) for this work; we need people who are generally chill and supportive of you, while still being real. How does it feel to just wear and have those things? Does it make you smile when folks comment or compliment you on them?

Now we move to people. As we've discussed elsewhere, the people you surround yourself with, your community, is part of your extended sense of self. If you don't feel that you have people who are good to and supportive of who you really are, then you don't have the right people in your life. As you continue the inner and outer work of manifesting your own gender, the people who are truly interested in you, who truly care about you, will stay around and become closer to you, and the ones who do not resonate will move away. Humans are complex and messy beings made of meat and dreams and hopes and trauma, and as such, those processes are likely to be uncomfortable and unpleasant, but hold on, because they are rewarding. Nothing makes you smile like a true friend, someone who truly believes in you and supports you and loves you for who you are.

Each of these things that you've worked with, that you've considered, those are all building blocks of your gender. There's another aspect of this to explore also: your actual, physical body. Many trans people seek medical intervention to make their inner parts match their outer parts. Unfortunately, because of the cissexist assumptions that we are raised in, we often assume that the body parts we want are the ones that are socially associated with the gender that we identify with. Sometimes they are; sometimes they are not, and the cisgender narrative follows logic like, "Women have vaginas, therefore all women would want a vagina." This isn't true, regardless of whether someone is cisgender or transgender; I know plenty of trans girls who are happy with their girl dick and trans guys who are fine with their man vaginas (even calling them "girl dick" and "man vagina" suggests that there's a lot of unpacking our culture has to do relating to reproductive organs and gender). There are quite a few nonbinary people who aren't interested in any kind of physical transition at all; they are quite happy as they are and don't require any physical alteration to make themselves—you guessed it—smile.

For some people, the medical aspects of transition are linked to social dysphoria/euphoria: "I want to be seen as a woman, and these are body parts that make people see someone as a woman in our society." That is a real and valid reason. For some trans people, medical transition stems from a felt physical sense of wrongness at their current configuration or rightness about another one. The "born in the wrong body" narrative has a lot of problems with it, but at its core, it is a way that a lot of trans people express the physical felt sense of wrongness with their reproductive and sexual characteristics.

If all of that seems too cerebral, let me break it down for you with personal examples: I am a woman, but I'm also nonbinary. While *woman* fits for most situations, and in fact there is a part of me that feels centered in that identity, there is a part of me that does not, and that part of me feels agender, larger than human gender and not something that fits into those categories. So I'm both a woman and a not-a-woman.

I'm also transfeminine; I was assigned male at birth and have had physical medical alterations to my body as well as social alterations to make me fit in community in ways that feel more right to me.

Those are ways that I find my smiles. Your ways to gender euphoria and manifesting yourself in the world may be entirely different, and that is good and valuable too.

Safety

I would like to name here that being able to play with your gender presentation is a privilege not everyone has. Given the endemic cultural hatred toward people who defy gender norms, doing things to alter your appearance and presentation can put your job, family connections, friendships, and life at risk.

This is part of the reason that the idea that trans people "become" trans for some kind of spurious popularity is complete bunk: being out as yourself while trans isn't safe. We may face different types and degrees of difficulty as a result of our presentation and how much (and who) we challenge by dint of being ourselves, but at the end of the day, it isn't safe for anyone.

The reason that it is not safe has nothing to do with messing around with gender, which is in and of itself as safe as buttons. The lack of safety comes from the reactions of cisgender people who may disapprove. I want everyone to be themselves, but sometimes you can only fully be yourself in a limited circumstance, and I also want everyone to be safe.

It's important to build a good safety network and community, which I touched on a little in the previous chapter. Making sure that you have people who support you being yourself regardless of how you express your gender is invaluable. Finding ways to ease into things, practice, and engage in bits of this work around supportive people is often the way we have to go.

Increased visibility of transgender people without increased education and humanization has led to increased violence and hostility toward people who don't conform to the binary or who are otherwise perceived as transgender. Some of us come out because we feel safe and present a brave face to the world to try and help make it safer for others, but that does not need to be you if you do not feel ready. Your safety comes first, always; if you are not ready to come out or be fully public as trans or nonbinary, please take your time and live to trans another day. You matter to more people than you realize.

EXERCISE: HEART, CENTER, AND GUT TEST

Your body has wisdom that your head does not. This exercise helps you tap into that wisdom in a direct way when it comes to whether or not something connects to you, resonates for you, or is right for you. All of the places where I mention the Smile Test above can also be put through the Heart, Center, and Gut Test.

Our brains and minds are super complex; when you ask a person about any particular issue, they could have a dozen different thoughts, each leading to a dozen different conclusions. For someone who is easily overwhelmed (like me) or who easily overthinks things (like me), this test can also be invaluable. It's also helpful for when the Smile Test doesn't work; sometimes nothing brings you to smile, but there are still options that are closer to your self and your nature.

To perform the Heart, Center, and Gut Test, take a few deep breaths, forcing yourself to slow your breathing and breathe through your nose, if possible. Deep breathing triggers the para-sympathetic nervous system, and we want that to be active during this process.

Once you have breathed and centered a bit, do a body scan. Starting with your head, take a breath to feel how each part of your body feels. If it is tense, try and relax it a bit on the exhale. For the time being, we are just noting and relaxing.

Once you have worked your way from your head down to your feet, bring your attention back to your heart. Then think about the subject in question. Breathe. Try to experience how your heart and chest feel. Remember how it felt when you were doing the body scan? How does it feel now in comparison? Is it tense or uneasy? Does it feel light and giddy? Calm and settled? Think about that, and then move on.

Take a few more deep breaths and relax your chest, and then draw your attention down to your solar plexus. Again, bring the subject to mind. Again, pay attention to how you feel: tense or relaxed, excited or restrained, calm or nervous. Compare it to how you felt when you passed this area earlier.

Take a few more breaths and relax your solar plexus, then turn your attention to your gut. Feel down in the base of you, in the deepest places where the light does not reach. Again, think about the subject. How does your gut feel? Do you feel a bit queasy or do you feel settled? Are there butterflies or scorpions in your stomach? How does the physicality of the deepest center in your body react to this thought? Again, compare it to how it felt when you did your first scan.

Take a few breaths and relax your gut, and then a few more breaths and relax your whole body again. Think about the differences between when you did your body scan and when you introduced the subject to those various centers of your body. Compare the experiences. Does your body like this idea? Does one part feel differently from the others? If so, feel free to revisit all the parts and even spend some time focusing on that part, reintroducing the idea again or perhaps a different subject or option instead and seeing the difference.

We just checked with various centers of your body on how you felt about a particular thing and used our conscious mind to help figure out how you on a physical level, at the base, feel about it. This knowledge can be a bit murky, but it is your body's holy wisdom. As C. S. Lewis puts it in his polytheist epic *Till We Have Faces*, "Holy wisdom is not thin and clear like water, but thick and dark like blood."[14] Your conscious mind can help you come to clear decisions about what you find in the darkness of your body, and in this way you can ensure that all parts of you are on board with a particular thing. If not, ask yourself why, and that can help you explore further depending on how you want to handle it and its importance to you. If this is about gender and attributes associated with gender, it can help you more easily pick up on sources of dysphoria and euphoria, and may even be able to help you tease out why the subject causes those feelings (though remember, when it comes to gender, those feelings are valid for you whether or not you understand them).

---

14. Clive Staples Lewis, *Till We Have Faces* (Orlando, FL: Harcourt & Brace, 1980), 50.

As another note, don't worry about your conscious thoughts when checking in with your heart, center, and gut—those will likely be all over the place. Your mind has lots of opinions, but we aren't asking your mind right now; we are asking your body. Your body is how you manifest in this world at this time; it is your base of operations in this incarnation and an essential part of who you are in this life. Its wisdom should be respected and honored in a way that brings you to a place of harmony and good health.

Who Are You?

We can start here with this famous and important question: Who are you?

Deep in meditation with Dionysos and Ariadne after a wild, ecstatic dance and worship session, I spoke to them about gender. I talked to them about who I was and how I saw myself. This was early in deepening my relationship with them, and I wanted to make sure that they accepted me before I went any deeper.

I talked to them about gender and how many trans people unpack it these days. "I know myself to be a woman. So I am. That's how we look at it. We call it self-identification."

"Yes. Yes." Came the response in the vision. "We love this, yes. You know yourself to be who you are. You are who you know yourself to be. We love this."

One of the cores of the Mysteries of Dionysos that I connect to is self-knowledge; through his transformative path, through Ariadne's labyrinth, we may come face-to-face with his Mirror, the spirit that reflects, that we seek ourselves in and see ourselves in. Knowing yourself is at the heart of his Mysteries. Of course

Ariadne and he would support an understanding of yourself that says you are who you know yourself to be, not the illusion that others project onto you.

So who are you?

What is your gender?

You don't have to go deep right now; we'll get there. What do you call yourself? *Man, woman, nonbinary?* Any of the other identities we listed at the beginning of this book or that you've found elsewhere?

If you are a bit unsure, it's not a big deal. Pick one that appeals to you. Pick one that makes you feel interesting in a good way. Pick one that makes you smile when you imagine people calling you that.

Now we get to explore what makes that up!

Elements

Pagans love their elements. There are a whole lot of elemental schemes in the world, but the classical Greek, four-elemental theme (at least, the version that has become popular, there were multiple ancient takes) is the one that we're going to work with in this book, mostly because it's familiar to many people. Feel free to find ways to apply these principles to other elemental or spiritual organizational schemes that you appreciate.

The classical Western, four-element scheme was first proposed by Empedocles, a Greek magician, mystic, philosopher, prophet, and self-proclaimed living god, who associated the four elements with four deities: fire with Zeus, air with Hera, earth with Pluton, and water with Nestis (Persephone). Aristotle associated qualities of hot and cold, dry and wet to the elements. (Fire is hot and dry, air is hot and moist, earth is cool and dry, water is cool and moist.) These are conceptual qualities but have long shaped the way these elements are approached in Western spiritual systems. Aristotle added another element, aither, which has been translated as "brightness" and was considered the matter in which the heavenly bodies hung (but was also in some systems considered the purest, clearest form of "fire").

The idea of the elements is that these substances, or the energies they manifest as, are the building blocks of the world. There have been comparisons made with the states of matter (earth and solid, water and liquid, air and gas, fire and plasma), but also with building blocks of human realities and spirits.

If we are going to honor your gender or lack thereof, we have to know it. We have to know its shape or the shape that the lack of it makes. We have to understand what that means, what that looks like. To understand that, we have to know what it's made of. We as human beings are composite entities, unable to survive without the mitochondria in our cells (which are their own beings and do not have human DNA), the gut bacteria that helps us break down our food, and numerous other creatures living in and around the environs of our bodies. Many also believe in a multipart soul. Having many parts can still mean a whole thing; we just want to look at the parts to know what we are working with.

So many trans and nonbinary people spend their lives trying to understand these things. This isn't a simple task; this is the beginning of the journey for some and another step in the journey for a great many other people who will be reading this.

But how do we find what those elements are? I have some exercises both mundane and magical to help us tease out some details. The exercise "Phanes and the Mirror" is there to kick-start the process spiritually, and while the other exercises may seem more mundane in scope, remember the principles of animist practice: things need to be addressed on all levels, spiritual as well as emotional, mental, and physical. I encourage you to attempt all of these exercises, as all of them can potentially bear good fruit.

EXERCISE: PHANES AND THE MIRROR

For this exercise, what you will need is a mirror, something to cover the mirror with like a veil or piece of cloth, and a candle. Some incense is good to use as an offering to the powers involved.

Cover the mirror with the veil. Turn your back to the mirror. Light the incense and recite these words inspired by the Orphic Hymn to Protogonos (the firstborn, all-gendered being also called Phanes, who is reborn in Zagreus and Dionysos).[15]

Say:

> *Erikipaios, ineffable, of hidden revolutions, scion shining on all,*
>
> *O being who wipes the dark mist away from eyes,*
>
> *Bearing the holy light, for this I call you Revealer*

---

15. Apostolos N. Athanassakis and Benjamin M. Wolkow, trans., *The Orphic Hymns* (Baltimore, MD: John Hopkins University Press, 2013), 8.

I call you Unveiler
I call you Radiance
I call you Phanes

Turn out the light. Be there in the darkness and connect to it. In the darkness things are unformed, unshaped; we cannot see what they are. Allow that to be the case, as you do not know who or what you are. Allow yourself to be unknown.

Imagine an egg in the darkness, a vague shape you can make out, and witness it shake as a serpentine shape coils around it and squeezes it. If you are not someone who does visualization well, imagine it conceptually, or what the kinesthetic boundaries of something like that might feel like.

A crack forms in the egg and light spills out.

Say:

I call you Radiance!

Open your eyes. Light the candle.

As the candlelight fills the space, imagine the egg cracking. Bursting forth from it is a winged being, pure light, pure potential, all genders and species and bodies. Set the candle down so that it is in front of you (and will be behind your back when you turn toward the mirror).

Say:

I call you Revealer!

Turn around toward the mirror.

Say:

> I call you Phanes! Wipe the dark mist away from my eyes! Remove the veil so that I may see and know my true self.

And pull the veil off of the mirror.

Look at the shapes in the mirror as you breathe deeply. Do not focus on any one thing, take it all in. Use no judgment, but consider what you feel about what you see, what images and thoughts cross your mind.

Say:

> Hail to the Mirror, sacred Toy and tool. As Phanes has unveiled me, I ask you to reflect the truth of my deepest self to me.

Continue to gaze into the mirror while you breathe. If you wish, you can continue to call on Starry Phanes, Protogonos (firstborn), or the Mirror to remove the veils between you and a vision of yourself, to show you your deepest truth.

Do not focus too tightly on what you see or don't see. Take in shapes. Take in feelings. A visual mirror is the gateway to the Mirror spirit, but visual cues are not the source of every piece of understanding here. Breathe and consider what you feel, what you see, and what thoughts come across your mind. Feel the center of your body as you breathe and observe how it reacts. Your heart and gut know your truth already; we are just getting your mind on board.

Ask again, "Who am I?"

See how you feel. If you are frustrated, ask yourself why. Are you frustrated because you feel like you aren't learning anything new? Then ask yourself, "What do I already know?"

Take in your feelings, random images that come to mind, words or songs that you think, smells, or considerations. Each time something comes up that feels significant, hold it in your mind while taking a breath in and out and focusing on your heart and your center and gut. Do these things feel solid in there? Do they feel exciting, as though they have been bound and are now freed? Do they feel wrong or like they don't sit well? Think about each of these things.

Then take the candle and place it in front of the mirror so it is between you and the mirror.

Ask again, "Who am I?"

Look in the mirror at what has been revealed to your eyes, but again, try not to focus too much on any one thing. Take it all in and see what filters through your mind, your heart, your gut, your senses. Absorb and consider each thing. Again, any time any thought or idea feels particularly charged, hold that thought and breathe in and out, focusing on how your heart and gut feel.

Do this until you are ready to be done. Thank Phanes, the Revealer, the Unveiler, and thank the Mirror, who helps us to see our true selves. Blow out the candle and return to reality.

Write about your experience. Which ideas gave you especially strong feelings? What were those feelings? Write all of that down. Pass these through the Smile Test: which of those things, if you say them about you, make you smile? If they don't make you smile, how do they make you feel?

In this exercise, you called on the primordial all-gendered god and the spirit of the sacred Mirror of Dionysos to help you have a deeper understanding of yourself. We are trying to find the concepts, the words, the definitions, the ideas, the feelings and, beneath them, the spiritual shapes that resonate most deeply with you, that connect the most powerfully to your deepest nature and sense of self.

Keep a list of the things that resonate the most powerfully with you. Those things are things that we can incorporate into later exercises and other parts of the work going forward.

EXERCISE: IF MY GENDER WAS A MIXTURE OF ELEMENTS, WHAT WOULD IT BE?

Now we can play with the classical elements! I'd like you to consider the attributions that the classical elements have as well as the elements themselves.

Most people have one or more elements they strongly identify with, whether it's because you think it's cool (fire is cool, come on), because you think it's practical and solid (like earth), fluid and beautiful (like water), free-spirited and brilliant (like air), or unaligned and absent, or for many other reasons. I am 100 percent sure that if I asked you your favorite element you would have one or more answers (or if you're like me, you would try and explain why each is most important to you and then follow up with the one you like the most).

Regardless, I want you to take the element that you feel most connected to and ask yourself why you do and what it means to you. What is it to be fiery and why is that a good thing? What is earthiness and how does it make you feel more secure? Explore your feelings about those elements and that self-identification.

Come up with three key words about that favorite element (or elements, because I know some of you will have more than one) that you love. Imagine someone using those words or concepts for you and feel it in your heart and center. Imagine them being used for you and see if they make you smile. Listen to your body on this one; it has important things to say.

Now, to take this to a spiritual level, consider spiritual entities you associate with that element. The classical elements of Empedocles have deities connected to them. All of these deities are ones with admittedly complex ancient stories about them and were likely not universally viewed in the past the way pop culture and mass media have reduced them in the present. You can think of them as gods of those elements. If you think of other deities or powerful spirits who you are comfortable connecting to that you relate to those elements instead, I encourage you to follow both your instincts and whatever spiritual guidance you may have on it.

You can take some of your key words and compose a prayer to that deity or spirit who you associate with that element, asking them to help you understand and embody those elements in a healthy way.

For example, I love earth. I love its solidity and reliability, I love its fruitfulness and expansiveness, and I love its magnanimous nature and strength. I associate earth with Kybele first in my personal practice (though there are many gods who fit the bill). So taking those things, I would compose a prayer that says something like,

> *Oh Kybele, Mother of the Gods, all-nurturing god-dess of the earth, help me to be strong and unbreak-able like the mountain, prosperous and abundant as the fertile valley; help me to have much so I can give much, all in line with my highest good.*

These individual attributes, these bits and pieces that make us up, are worthy of being honored and supported. They are holy. It is rightful to ask for support in them and for connection between them and greater spiritual powers. Crafting a prayer or affirma-tion around these will be good practice for other work that we will be doing around the elements of gender.

Once you have done this with the classical elements, you can consider other elements, aspects, or features of nature that you are drawn to: light, darkness, thunder, lightning, volcanoes. Consider their features and run them through the same processes. Are there deities or spirits you associate those qualities with? Compose a similar prayer regarding those qualities as well.

EXERCISE: NAMES, PRONOUNS, TITLES, ROLES

While our gender identities may be personal and highly internal, how we are treated and addressed in the world is part of our social sphere. It is possible for there to be a big divide between who you are and how you are addressed, and that is frequently a dysphoric situation. Consider how much better it would be if who you are and how you are addressed matched.

If you're having trouble figuring those things out (and even if you aren't, it can't help to explore), here is an exercise to help you really consider what ends up fitting you best.

We've already talked a little bit about pronouns and figuring those out for you. Like names, that can be a lifelong process, something that evolves and changes over time as your understanding of yourself and the context around those names and pronouns change.

But right now we just want a list of these to work with. Write down a list of all of the names, pronouns, and titles or positions that have been given to you (that you feel comfortable writing down). (If you have a dead name or dead pronouns, please don't hurt yourself with them; nobody needs that. We already know that those things aren't you!)

Titles and positions can be things like "manager" or things like "artist," descriptors for things that you *are* because of things that you *do*.

Go down the list and do the Heart, Center, and Gut Test and the Smile Test, imagining someone calling you these things. Ask yourself how they feel in your heart and center when you breathe through them, and if they make you smile when you imagine them applied to you. Which ones pass each one? Check them off and notice which ones get the best and strongest reactions. Those are more potential elements.

Now you probably have multiple lists of attributes, styles, images, thoughts, elements, names, and titles available to work with. Put down all of the results of these prior exercises that resonated well and connected well with you—any of them that passed the Smile Test and the Heart, Center, and Gut Test. Now the next question to ask is, what to do with them?

Some or many of these pieces will naturally weave themselves together and be associated for you already. The fact is, though, they don't need to be connected with each other or even make sense outside of their context. The reality is that both your body and your conscious mind agree these are things that resonate deeply with you, whether you understand why that is or not, and whether or not they make sense in connection to one another.

Now, I'd like you to take a close look at that list and ask yourself, which of these things are traditionally associated, in your culture, with masculine things? Which are associated with feminine things? Remember, you made this list without those attachments; you didn't choose these things because people consider them "masculine" or "feminine"; you chose these things because your heart, body, and mind were in alignment with them. Remember also that those values of masculine and feminine are things that shift from place to place and culture to culture.

In fact, if you are a woman and that is where your gender sits, then those are women's things. If you are a man and that's where you feel solid, those are men's things. They aren't women's or men's things because of a vague, uncodified social definition of those things. They are men's things and women's things because you are a man or a woman, and those are your things, things that are part of you.

So if you look at this collection of traits, mostly traits that people associate with gender, as a whole, what picture does it give you? Can you find a solid theme? A cohesive narrative that ties most of those parts together?

If you can find a theme, an aesthetic, a category, how does that fit with the way you described yourself in the very first exercise in the book (where we asked you to describe your gender without using *man/woman*, *masculine/feminine*, *boy/girl*)? Does it match that description or intersect with it in any way? Does that change your answer to the original question? Remember, no right or wrong answers here, just things to look at and consider.

These basic and powerful elements of you are things that are deeply attached to your identity and sense of self, and as we've discussed, gender identity is a way of categorizing or describing that identity and sense of self. These, therefore, are elements of your gender.

I challenge you to find a single one among those that has no precedent in a sacred context meaningful to you. Gods and spirits and Ancestors are often described with aesthetics, wearing certain clothing, having certain roles, associating with different classical elements, stars, and constellations. There is nothing that is an element of you that is not reflected in that which is sacred and holy. Every part of you, every piece, can be blessed and honored, as it is now, as it was before, and however it changes over time.

Your love of hats is reflected by Odin and your fiery nature by Loki. Your magical singing voice was shared by Orpheus and Sappho. Your love of beauty is shared by Freyja and Aphrodite. Your care for the wounded can be seen in the reflection of Dian Cécht, of Airmid, of Asklepios and Hygeia. Your desire to protect may be witnessed by Apollon, and your desire to hunt by his sister, Artemis.

When we break gender down into elements like this, free from the trappings and considerations of the oppressive gendered systems that humans have created to control one another, we find that it is made of qualities that are seen in our sacred values and beings. How, then, are our genders not also sacred?

Gender isn't sacred when it is used as a tool of oppression, but that isn't about gender, is it? That's about oppression. Race and ancestry are also used as tools of oppression, but anyone who thinks that any racial category is inherently less sacred because of its ancestry is flat-out incorrect.

If you wouldn't say that someone, or a part of someone, is less sacred because of disability, because of race, because of any other inherent quality that they do not choose, then why would they be less sacred because of their gender and how they choose to embrace and present it? Gender is deeply personal. It is between you and yourself, it is between you and those you choose to share it with, and it is made of what you are made of.

And what you are made of is sacred and is reflected in the stars. You are also a child of Earth and Starry Heaven. I'll share some modern liturgy based on the Orphic burial texts that has been inspiring to me:

> And when you come upon the waters of memory the guardians of the underworld will rise up and challenge you and they will ask, "Who are you?"
>
> And you will reply, "I am a child of Earth and Starry Heaven, but I descend from Heaven alone. This you yourselves know. I am Starry and my

*name is Starry and my people are Starry. I am pure
and I come from the pure."*

Journaling

What do you think of breaking down gender into recognizable
elements? Where have you incorporated various elements or
removed them from your life before? Is there a disparity between
the elements of your gender all put together and your whole
self-image? If so, where does that come from?

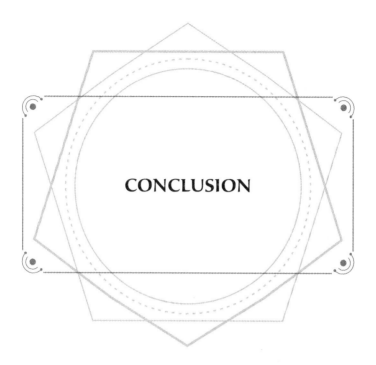

CONCLUSION

NOW THAT WE'RE AT the end of this work, you may still be saying to yourself, "I don't think what she's talking about here is gender."

And, in a way, you're right.

There is a sacred truth to you, a sacred reality that transcends this moment of linear time and transcends the life of your body and the universe that you witness every day. That sacred truth lies beneath both your body and your mind, subtle and hard to see for all the constructions and obstructions that have been placed in front of it.

Transgender people wrestle with the truth of themselves as we witness it being denied in every context of our lives. Can we be who we say we are if everyone else says that we are not? Yes, not only can we be who we say we are, we can't help but be that. How others treat us shapes how we present to the world—it does for everyone. But for trans folks, admission of our genders defy human law and custom in Western society. We bear the brunt of others' confusion and hurt, and we do it because we see a greater truth within us than has been granted to us.

Across the world, across cultures, we are known to be magical. We are the people of the Mirror; we have seen into our own souls, past the trappings placed on us by others. Those trappings get in the way of seeing your own soul and knowing yourself. *Man* and *woman*, *masculine* and *feminine*, are ways that we describe that reality, but they are not the reality itself, because they are words that we use for sets of qualities. They are real and can be holy, but if you are a man or a woman, you are a man or a woman for a reason, and that reason lies in a deeper place than *man* or *woman*.

In that darkness of the cave, the womb of the Mother, the place where you cannot see but can only be, you can know the truth of yourself. And if, when shared with other humans, that truth is described as *man* or *woman* or both, then that is good and holy too. And if you find something is not *man* or *woman*, then that is good, holy, true, and valid also.

For many, gender gets in the way of witnessing yourself. *Man* and *woman* carry expectations that force us to squeeze what we see one way or another. For those of us who are more used to navigating around gender, we see the glimmer of the light beneath it.

If you think that at the end this isn't really about gender, you aren't entirely wrong. This is about the sacred, about the divine within you, and the sacred and divine without. I have provided you with tools and thoughts and suggestions for ways to help you find the sanctity in your own gender so that you can find that sanctity in the things bigger than you.

In Dionysos's youth, his famous Toys were originally given to him because they were the sacred objects used by humans in ritual and to honor the gods: the Sphere or Ball, the Knucklebones or Dice, the Wheel, the Bull-roarer, the Spinning Top or Pinecone, the Rattle, the Posable Doll, the Tuft of Wool, the Golden Apple, and the Mirror. All represent sacred tools of humanity used in highest ritual. Gender is a sacred and powerful tool far too often used to harm, and above all else, I want people to be able to use it as a Toy, a thing of play, of joy, of connection, of training, a way to understand—a Toy that not everyone needs (even if in our society everyone needs to navigate it in some way).

Many trans folks feel cut off from the divine because we are taught not to see ourselves in it, while cis people are well-repre-sented in major and minor religions alike. Given some of the cor-rections that were attempted by second-wave feminism and the influence of that movement on the broader Pagan movement, it is almost inevitable that transgender people are made to feel unwel-come in many Pagan spaces. That school of feminist thought was one of the origin points of the idea of trans women as abusers and rapists, as men trying to sneak into women's spaces and steal their power. How sadly ironic that people who would seek liber-ation for all women would villianize some of the most margin-alized among us merely to have another demon to rail against; their arguments against trans women's existence follow the same template that both their earlier feminist predecessors and conser-vative Christians use against lesbians being treated with dignity and given equal rights.

It is important that transgender and nonbinary people know that they are sacred, holy, whole, wholesome, and healers. It is important that we know we have support, love, and guidance from greater powers than us who see through the maze of flesh and society to our true selves burning like the Starry flames that they are underneath.

The treatment of trans people by modern society as abominations, as diseased, as confused, as predators is an aberration in human history. Through time, other human beings have recognized our holiness, our power, and our ability to heal. We transform the narrative to bring forward the liminal, to show humanity the things that may be missed, forgotten, and lost for other reasons, or because humanity has closed our doors and walls and selves to greater things. Transgender people cross boundaries by our existence; we defy the false reason and laws of humanity and speak to a primal, deeper truth—one deeper than words, one deeper than laws, one deeper than society and civilization.

Because of that inherent defiance, so central to our natures, we are vilified in places where control and oppression are glorified, in places where the domination of other human beings based on anatomical features and ancestry are considered a given part of the truth of the world. We stand out as exceptions and are even exceptions to ourselves, for no one of us can contain all that we are, and no one of us has the power to change the others. We are visible manifestation of a magic that runs through every human bloodline, a spirit that calls to the voice of nature, of the earth, of the Mother, of Kybele.

We are wonder-workers and shape-shifters; our sense of self is often fluid and is matched by our shifting appearances. We are put into one place in life, a place that our societies consider immutable, and whether through the magic of clothing, the magic of words, the magic of medicine and herbs, or the magic of our wills alone, we transform ourselves in their minds and ours and try and bring forward the deeper, sacred truths about ourselves into an often unreceptive world. That shape-shifting, that wonder-working, is powerful and potent. While cisgender people can be and do those things at times, transgender people do those things by our very nature. We have perspective, value, and understandings that are unique to us, and yes, again, we are holy, sacred, healthy, whole, and wholesome.

If you consider yourself cisgender (the same gender you were assigned at birth) and you have walked through the exercises that I provide in this book and have explored the places that have been revealed, congratulations, you have done a tiny portion of the work that any transgender or nonbinary person does as part of daily existence. You have gotten a glimpse into some of the places that we go to understand ourselves, and you, too, have come away changed. What do you plan to do with it? Where do you plan on taking it? Hopefully you will come away with an understanding of not only the sacred links between identity, gender, and the divine, but also with a deeper understanding of and appreciation for the rich lives of transgender people. And with that, a comprehension of our struggles as we navigate in societies that are far too often made to crush opposition, nonconformity, and, in the end, our spirits. I hope that understanding will serve you well in supporting transgender people in your mundane and spiritual communities; let that be one of your takeaways. My people belong, and in fact, having spiritual practice and community where we are not enthusiastically welcomed is trying to have a spiritual practice or community that cuts off a vital and powerful part of humanity and the human experience. If transgender people aren't as sacred to you as your "mothers and fathers," or however you binarize the Ancestors, then you are not only ignoring a large part of the human story, but also turning your back on the blessings of many of the gods and spirits that have been linked to us through human history.

If you're transgender or nonbinary and reading this, I first want to say that I hope the exercises produced no dysphoria in you, and I apologize if they did. Again, I never want one of my kin to put themselves through anything harmful when they do not need to. Next, I will ask: What has this taught you about yourself? What have you learned about your own gender and the divine parts of you? What links have you found between yourself and the greater sacred realities of the universe, and what paths have opened to you as a result? I dearly hope that this work helps you to see and understand the value in yourself—and not just value and validity, but also your connection to the sacred, the origin, the end, the cycle, the light and dark, elements and stars, and every other sacred part of reality. If I have helped you find even a glimpse of that connection, of the potential guidance and support that you can receive from your spiritual allies—and even more, if it gave you a glimpse of hope for a world where our natures are as revered as everyone else's—I will be satisfied with the result.

Finally, if you started considering yourself the gender you were assigned at birth, and in the reading of this book have discovered a deeper truth, congratulations! I am glad you've found that, and again, that is another purpose of this writing. Too often meager words and hidebound ideas prevent us from connecting to our deeper natures and truths. Regardless of what you call yourself afterward or what steps you take, you are going to be a greater person than you were before. Now you know more about yourself and can connect to that part also, both within and without, both in the Earth and in Starry Heaven, on all levels of the great tree, the great mountain, that connects all things. Even if you never engage in nonbinary or trans society, never pick up a flag or find one of the names that we use for ourselves, you will have *transcended* not only who you are but also the restrictions society has placed on you. You have shattered chains in your mind and in yourself. What are you going to do with your newfound freedom? I hope, as I do with everyone else reading this work, that you will embrace the inner parts of yourself and find ways to bring them out in the most blessed and healthy ways possible for you. May you live a free life, a healthy life, a holy life, knowing better than anyone who you are.

Actually, most of those wishes apply to everyone reading this. I dream of a time when the masks come off—not the ubiquitous masks we've found to protect ourselves against plague (I am in full support of those kinds of masks)—but the masks that we wear not because we were born with them, not because we chose them, but because they were put on our faces as infants and we were never told that we were able to take them off. Beneath that mask is your real face. As a follower of Dionysos and Ariadne and Kybele and other gods whose practices are ecstatic, I know that in the wildness of dance, of sex, of song, of laughter, of the things that bring you outside of yourself, you begin to sweat, and in that sweat, that sacred lubricant, that mask placed on you at birth can start to slip. And it's terrifying when it does; it feels like your skin is coming off!

It's not your skin, though. If you've done enough of this work, you know that there is something under that mask, skin waiting desperately to breathe and feel the wind and the light of sun and moon and stars. And these heavy clay masks we wear are what are keeping us from feeling those things and connecting at the deepest levels with the sacred powers that they represent: our Ancestors, our gods, our spirits, the living spirit of that-which-is.

Underneath that mask could be anything. There could be a woman hidden under the mask of a man, or a man hidden under the mask of a woman. There is a star, and there could even be whole constellations! What else is under there; what other wonders can you find beneath and bring forward in yourself? Do you find a great healer or hero? A face from the past reflected through time? A snake-haired monster, a bull-horned demigod, a wild wood nymph, a wise oracle? Once you begin to find shapes and layers, you can keep peeling, keep cleaning, and keep refining. As you clean the Mirror and gaze deeper and deeper into yourself, you find new shapes and forms to bring forward, each one closer to a whole understanding of yourself.

Now is a time that literal masks are being taken off. We've seen an attempted fascist coup of the United States and successful domination by similar governments across the world. The idea of there being a nobility in the tradition of the Western settler states has been undermined even to the people who most benefit from it by this unveiling (which is a literal translation of the word *apocalypse*). As they reveal their truths, as they say the quiet parts out loud, they grow emboldened, those that would place their boots on our necks, control our bodies, and twist our languages of liberation to use them as chains to reinforce their dominance, their hatred, their bigotry, and their power. They take off those literal masks perhaps as an unconscious symbol and certainly as a conscious way of saying, "We don't care. We don't care if you die. We don't care if we spread a plague or disease. We don't care if we die either; it's all worth it if it harms you." They use the word *own* ironically in these contexts: to "own" the libs or leftists or however they define their enemy, when in fact, at the base of it, their enemy is freedom: the freedom to be the person you are, to love the people you love, to find essential dignity in yourself and your Ancestors, to see yourself in the divine and see the divine in you. And even as the plague passes, as the demagogues are shut out, they put their masks back on, hoping we will forget what we've seen underneath. We can't allow that. We know the truth now; we should never forget and should use that knowledge to protect one another and our world in the future.

And this is part of why I write this work now and bring it forward now. More than ever in human history, we need people to be able to find the deeper spiritual truths and understandings of themselves and bring them into full, glorious manifestation. We need our healers and heroes, our demigods and our own loving monsters; we need our witches and nymphs and goblins. We need our stars. We need to know that those stars are inside each of us, that the rude clay masks placed on us at birth can be chipped and broken, can be loosened and dropped. Not only that we can, we must.

The world needs us now more than ever, with climate disaster looming, colonial states and the oppressive mentalities that reinforce them will continue to clamp down and tighten their punishing bindings. A common phrase you will hear from trans folks is "Our existence is resistance." We who choose to embody and embrace ourselves in the face of these things resist the narratives of oppression, patriarchy, capitalism, colonialism, and racism that would reduce us to the functions of our reproductive organs or our ability to produce work for the benefit of those we will never meet.

Gender is the beginning of that for many people. The first time that most trans and nonbinary people realize how toxic many of the dominant narratives are is when they first embrace themselves and see the way the world reacts (though to be fair, most people who aren't white in Western societies already have a very good understanding of that regardless of gender). We say, "This is who I am," and the resistance and violence turned on us shows the weakness and sickness of the narratives that would deny it, and also the inherent danger. Those who are cornered fight the hardest, and most of the people who engage deliberately in violent and oppressive behavior against transgender and nonbinary people do not realize that they are acting merely as a vector for a greater disease, a social sickness that reduces people to their visible body parts and abilities to produce.

Anyone seeking their true gender, their true sense of self in themselves, in other humans, in nature, and in the cosmos helps to start breaking the weakest links of those chains. How much more powerful could that freedom be were we to stop compromising who we are entirely?

I believe that in each human being is the capacity for stunning goodness and brightness. I believe that most humans, when exposed to empathy in one way or another, will try to make choices to make the world better for others. Society may punish them for it, and their reactions are their own, but when you realize that in every other person is a beating heart and living mind and divine spirit, it becomes hard to live in such a way that disregards the well-being of them entirely.

I think that the work of finding the sacred connections between yourself and the cosmos, as well as the sacred connections between yourself and other human beings, is vital to the health of humanity and to overcoming the darkest and most dangerous parts of the age that we live in. And gender is one of the places where the gap is bridged, as we see reflections of it in the elements and the stars, in other human beings, and also in ourselves.

So no, this book is not just about gender, but gender is a powerful key to unlock the door to the understanding of yourself. In knowing yourself, you can know better ways to relate to the world and other people. In knowing yourself, you can find peace between yourself and your fate, and also discern the places where what you may once have thought was fate was instead a distraction or a chain placed on you by others. In knowing yourself, you can be free, and in being free, free to help liberate others too.

I would hope someday to see humanity brought to a level of spiritual awareness where they honor themselves individually and collectively. I want to see a world where humans treat everything as though it has a face (animism) because they know that a similar spark that dwells within them dwells within everything that exists. I wish to work toward a world where dignity and value are given to all things without them having a function in the creation of money or reinforcement of existing oppressive social mores.

That may or may not be a long way off, but until we know ourselves, we cannot be in right relationship with ourselves or anything else in the world. For too long, gender has been used to keep us from perceiving certain things about ourselves and the world. I would rather gender be used as a sacred tool (or Toy, and for me in many ways those things are the same) to enhance life and freedom. I know it can be; my people and I have been doing it for as long as humanity has existed. I would like people to see and understand the sacred shapes beneath it—the reason one gender or another or none fits us—and use it as a way to understand ourselves and our world.

As I mentioned earlier, but pertinent here: in a sacred rite to Dionysos and Ariadne, when lying in a trance after dancing myself to exhaustion, I asked them about trans and nonbinary people. "I have always had women like you in my service," Ariadne said, and it turned out to be true. But even more, they seemed exuberant at the idea of self-identification. "Yes," they said, "yes, you are who you know yourself to be. You are who you say you are."

In some ways, this is the core of how I understand some of their most powerful Mysteries. In every way, this is the core Mystery of what I am trying to convey here in this book: you are who you say you are. You are who you know yourself to be. Compulsory gender binds us so that we cannot perceive our own nature, and so I provide you with ways to peek underneath it to see the glory, the monster, the angel, the divinity, and the human being beneath. Mine are not the only ways, and possibly not even the best ways; please, find others too and share them also. We need this now more than ever.

The journey may start with gender, but it never ends. It will never end. May it never end for you and for all of us, because that journey is a journey to the gods, to spirit, to the divine. It is the journey home, to the home that we never left and is all around us if we can bring forth the part of ourselves that knows how to see it and knows how to dance in it. Gender can be a key for a lock, an oar for a boat, a sail for a ship in this journey of liberation and fulfillment. That journey is the human birthright; as you join with this flesh and open your eyes and cry out for the first time, you feel separation from your mother and from the Mother. But you never really leave the Mother; you are never really separate from her, from the progenitor, from the divinity that brought you forward.

This is the work of memory. It is the work of remembering who you are and where you came from, the work of unveiling your eyes before the Mirror, the work of descending back into the cave where you cannot see but can feel, where you cannot read but can know.

You are sacred, and you are Starry. You are pure and of the pure, and that includes your gender and the way you embrace and present yourself. Because you are at the center of that. Because the sacred web of creation has no center, and yet every point on it is another center. You are the center too because every star is at the center of the sky, and Ariadne's Corona Borealis, her own Starry crown, is made of lovely light, fire, and power and yet has no center either.

Blessings of my gods and yours on you, Starry one. Thank you for walking this path with me. May our paths meet again in bright and joyous and hopeful times, with our true faces exposed so that we can witness one another's stellar glory and know the sacredness in one another, in the world, and in ourselves.

Journaling

What has changed for you between when you picked up this book and now? How has your understanding of gender shifted? How has your understanding of yourself shifted? How has your understanding of the cosmos shifted?

Who are you? And what are you going to do about it?

APPENDIX
GENDER MAGIC

THE WORD *INITIATION* GETS used in a lot of spiritual contexts, so before we go into discussing this kind of ritual, I'd like to talk about what I mean when I'm referring to initiations. As someone who has served as an initiator-priestess in a spiritual tradition and someone who has gone through initiations related to other powers and traditions, I have strong opinions about the subject.

First off, one of the distinctions that I like to make is the difference between what I think of as *spirit initiations* and *lineage initiations*. They are both powerful and transformative experiences, but a spirit initiation is one that occurs without the direct intervention of other humans. It is between you and spirits and gods, and changes your relationships with them without necessarily changing your relationships with other humans.

On the other hand, a *lineage initiation* also has most of the same elements, with the additional quality of being administered or guided by other humans who have been through the same or similar. A lineage initiation brings you into relationship with a group of embodied and potentially ancestral humans; as such, it requires living humans to administer the actual rite for it. If no one does that, no one may recognize the change of status and identity that comes with that ritual. Lineage initiations are found in many different forms of spiritual practice from Eastern martial arts to Western Mystery traditions and Indigenous spiritual groups.

An initiation is an experience that changes everything, yourself included. There is a life before it and then a life after it, and that difference is marked by the experience. It is a transformation of yourself or a changed understanding of yourself that, to your perspective and possibly the perspective of others, changes your position in the world in relation to other things.

A spirit initiation can look like:

+ Deep in meditation, a god speaks to you and shows you a truth about yourself and your life that reveals the many ways that they have been working in your life. They claim you as one of their own, tell you that you have a specific relationship with them, and give you guidance for how to foster and embody that relationship going forward.

+ During a moment of crisis, a deity or group of spirits comes forward to support you. They recognize that you belong with them and extend their hands to save you. By accepting that help, you not only save your life or the lives of others, but also join with those who are helping you, and that connection becomes a major force in your life.

Many of the classical descriptions of powerful spiritual experiences of saints and converts to various faiths take the form of spirit initiations.

A lineage initiation can look like:

+ A spiritual group whose rites you have been attending says that they see you as a member of their community. They perform a ritual with you present where the spiritual powers that oversee that community as well as the living members of that community are called on to recognize that you are one of them.

+ A teacher leads you through a set of spiritual trials, challenges, or journeys that help you to recognize truths about yourself and the universe, and also introduces another framework to connect to the universe and interact with it. At the end of this teaching sequence, the teacher lets you know that you have passed and hold those truths within yourself, and you may now pass those truths on to others.

+ Being taught the principles of a religion and then having a ceremony confirming that you understand that religion and are in some way a part of it.

Despite the words that I use for it, there is a spiritual element to all initiations, even lineage initiations that don't involve religious communities. That tie is the Ancestors: even joining a fraternity or sorority puts you into lineage with the members of those groups who have come before. Those are now your Ancestors to interact with how you choose, but regardless of how you choose, you have a relationship with them.

Trans folks have their own initiations. One of the more popular bits of language that we see in trans culture these days is about "eggs" and "eggs cracking." An "egg" is a person who has not yet realized that they are trans or has not announced it in any way (they haven't come out, often even to themselves). It's interesting, by the way, to see the connection between the language used for the cracking of the human trans egg and the Orphic Egg of creation.

There is a moment that comes for most trans and nonbinary people when we look in the Mirror, face our reflections (whether literally or not), and say to ourselves, "I am X." (Where X is different from whatever gender has been assigned to you at birth.) This is a powerful and transformative moment. It doesn't always stick; sometimes that moment has to happen over and over again through the years, but each time we acknowledge to ourselves that we are not the gender we were assigned at birth, our eggs crack a little bit more.

This is an initiatory experience. Whether or not you ever come out to someone else, coming out to yourself permanently changes you. It means that you cannot ever look back on the gender you were assigned at birth and say, "This is me" with any degree of certainty. The ground beneath you has shifted with the shift of your own perspective on yourself.

Trans people also experience lineage initiations. The series *Pose* (which I recommend to everyone; it should be required watching) shows glimpses of how they functioned in drag and ballroom house culture. Mothers would take in and support their daughters in transition, bringing them into the culture and teaching them what they needed to know to be themselves and survive in a world that rejected who they were and how they saw themselves. Less formally, I've seen trans community rally around folks who have only recently come out, providing tips on dress, presentation, and navigating the cissexist world.

At the same time, the lack of social initiations in broader society for people living in new-to-them genders leads to a lot of difficulty for new trans folks. A lot of people don't know what to expect when coming out and don't have any community that acknowledges them. I know a lot of trans women who have been shunned by cis and trans community alike for not being feminine enough in presentation, appearance, or behavior. I have seen countless nonbinary people have a core part of themselves denied as well.

I think that a potential solution to this is performing initiations into gender. I know binary trans folks who have had the members of the mostly cisgender communities that they belong to (families, congregations, covens, temples, clubs, etc.), who identify with the same gender as they do, have birthday or transition parties for them. This can be a wonderful experience as other men or women in someone's community come forward to acknowledge their gender and support them in it.

It can also be a harmful experience, as the understandings of gender that individuals in that community have may be those that run counter to the person's experience or understanding of themselves. It can be used to reinforce harmful stereotypes that don't well fit the newly out trans person and aren't really a part of their self-image. The people participating in those ceremonies aren't usually deliberately trying to be harmful, but we know that intent isn't everything: whether or not you mean to break a plate or step on a friend's foot, the plate remains broken and the friend has been harmed.

I think there are ways for that kind of ceremony to be powerful and beneficial without being restrictive and reinforcing concepts of gender that are harmful to the trans people undertaking them. I think a lot of the time when folks are uncomfortable with that kind of thing, it's because it is crafted without an understanding of what it's like to be trans and go through social, medical, or other forms of transition. In short, if there are no other trans people in the community, or if the recipient's understanding of themselves isn't taken into account, these things can do more harm than good, and nobody does this stuff to be deliberately harmful.

Gender reveal parties have become very popular in the last decade and have been the target of a lot of discomfort from transgender and nonbinary folks for a lot of reasons. A gender reveal party is a party where the parents of a newly born or unborn child make a public declaration of what gender they expect that child to be based on the shape of their genitals. We can see where this is already based around cissexism: the idea that genitals determine a person's gender, the idea that being cisgender is the human default, and the assumption that beginning to enforce a particular gender on a child before they are born does not set them up for a lifetime of unfair expectations they did not ask for.

Also, just to be real, there are deep patriarchal issues with gender reveal parties. A gender reveal party has nothing to do with gender; it exists to announce the shape of a baby's genitals (sit with that idea for a minute and see if it makes you uncomfortable; it should) and to reinforce the idea of what reproductive role a person will take when they are still a baby (again, if this doesn't make you uncomfortable, I'd like you to sit with the implications of it for a minute).

So we have a ceremony meant to cement in the world the idea of a person's role in life and reproduction as well as a public announcement about their genitals when they are too young to consent to any of those things. It's no wonder they don't just make trans people uncomfortable! The whole idea is rooted in the concept of genitals shaping your identity, your personality, and your destiny, and also in the idea that it's fine to force those things on someone without their consent.

However, what about the idea of an adult gender reveal? The idea has been floated around Tumblr and actually resembles some of the gender initiations that I mentioned before. Someone comes to a new understanding of themselves and their gender, community gathers and acknowledges it publicly in some fashion, and people who are of that gender provide them with clothing, gifts, ideas, tips for navigating life, traditionally gendered activities that the person can participate in, and more. The recognition is affirming (and in this case, consensual!), and the community support is sorely needed, as most trans folks who come out need all the support they can get in an otherwise hostile society. Cisgender people have equivalent rites in many cultures, where they are acknowledged as an adult and as a woman or a man. Why shouldn't transgender people have access to the same kind of acknowledgment and support?

An adult gender reveal would definitely fit into a lineage initiation, being an in-person, physical rite that acknowledges the person's new status and brings them into alignment with other community members who share that status. While trans people do have connections to their Ancestors of Gender naturally through their own self-knowledge, a rite like this can only strengthen those bonds.

To tie what we've been talking about here together, most trans folks undergo something analogous to a spirit initiation: they recognize a difference in themselves brought about by internal seeking. They choose to claim that identity by speaking it aloud, even if just to themselves, and they walk forward into the world with a changed relationship to themselves and society.

That may be more than enough for some people, but others might benefit from having an "adult gender reveal" party or a gendered initiation, where they are recognized by people whose opinions matter to them, people who they deal with every day.

In addition, both of these models leave out potential steps to connect to these things spiritually, which is an important consideration for many of us. Given how often transgender and nonbinary people are rejected by their spiritual communities and congregations (and this applies just as much to Pagan denominations and groups as it does to the more dominant Christian groups and other religions), finding ways to weave our narratives into the faiths that have been created to exclude us is a natural step in trying to bring health and fullness both to ourselves and to our religious traditions.

But what would that look like?

Self-Initiation: Cracking the Egg

If you're trans, maybe you've already come out to yourself. That's often one of the most difficult moments in our journeys, that moment of looking at yourself and realizing that not only do the pieces not fit, you are starting to understand why they don't fit.

Whether or not you have come out to yourself, if you have a spiritual practice that involves deities and other spiritual powers, have you come out to them? Asked them for support and acceptance? While this is kind of the central theme of this book, that crucial moment of coming out tends to define our future interactions over and over and should have close attention paid to it.

For this rite, you'll need yourself and a mirror. It's also helpful to be close to whatever shrine you use for your spirit or deity work. I don't know what gods or Ancestor groups or other holy powers you work with, so I'm going to leave this outline a little fill-in-the-blanks for you.

Set the space and time. Ideally, you'll want some privacy for this and not to be rushed. Prepare the space by doing a little cleaning and neatening. Don't go overboard, just make the space more tolerable to you, even if it means throwing a sheet over some laundry or a mess (I don't judge; we've all been there, and some of us live there).

Do some kind of cleansing for yourself. Ideally, you should take some kind of shower or bath. Use whatever scents make you feel good about yourself, focusing on those that align with your gender or that are sacred to the gods or spirits you're about to address. Do whatever shaving or makeup or other things help you feel yourself too.

Get dressed. Remember, clothing is part of your body and self-image. Put on the things that make you the most euphoric, that help you to connect the most to yourself.

Spend a little time breathing. Simple box breathing (breathe in for a four count, hold for a four count, breathe out for a four count, hold empty for a four count, and repeat), or another deep breathing technique for a few minutes, will help to calm you down and assist you in your focus.

Light a candle and some incense (or an oil burner if you use one). Take a deep breath to steady yourself and begin to call to your divine powers.

For the Ancestors, you can say something like,

> I call on my Ancestors of blood and spirit, of [insert lineages here]. I call on the Ancestors of [insert gender here], all of those who came before me who understood themselves in the ways that I understand myself. I call on the Trans Dead, those who have come before me, shaped me, and paved the way for me to be myself in the world.

Name individual trans Ancestors too—any of the ones who inspired you or even just those that you know who you feel drawn to.

Call to the land itself. You can say something like, "I call on the land beneath my feet, the land that nurtures and sustains me, and the lands that I have walked through to come to this place and time in my life. Thank you for supporting me; I am made of you as surely as I am made of my Ancestors." If you are on colonized land and are a settler, you may wish to ask for appropriate blessings for the original inhabitants of the land as well as their living descendants.

Since we tend to deal with deities more individually than collectively, it's harder to create a sample invocation, but if you speak up, they will listen. Call to any who matter to you, any who are represented on your shrines, any you regularly call or offer to, and any others who you feel you would like some form of support from. If you are at all concerned that you may not receive support from your gods, feel free also to call to any of the deities listed in the trans gods section.

If you can, pour out an offering to those who you've called; it's polite to give guests something to drink, and it can be as simple and universal as water or as fancy as you like.

Now that you've got everyone's attention, you can say something like,

> Greetings to all who have been assembled. I call you here today to let you know that my life is changing and to seek support in that. For many years, I was known as [list the name that you used before, the pronouns you used before, and the gender that people knew you as]. I have come to realize that these things are not the

truth of who I am. I ask you to set aside these under-standings of me; know that I have the same heart and mind and spirit, but I do not wish to be addressed and known in the same way as I was before. Please hold the knowledge of those former parts of me in sacred trust; prevent them from being revealed against my will should the time come that I do not wish them to be known.

All you who have come to me here, know that my name is [insert name], and I would like to be referred to as [insert pronouns] henceforward. I understand myself as [insert gender], which to me means [at this point, describe your gender].

(If you've been doing the exercises in the book, you may have more descriptors available, especially the elements. If you can't think of anything, just say the word that means your gender to you or say that you understand yourself as having none.)

Ancestors of [your gender], those who understand themselves as I do, please be here with me and help to guide my life going forward in all the ways that will be best for me. Know that I am also [your gen-der], hear me, see me, acknowledge me, and accept me as one of your own. Help me to step into my new role seamlessly and easily, and help those who share this identity with me to see it in me and acknowledge and honor it too.

Trans Ancestors: I am one of your children! I am one of your kin. You came before me and made the world ready for my coming. You came before me, and yet you shaped me in my life. You have walked these roads and similar before. Hear me, see me, accept me as one of your own, and stand behind me and beneath me; support me and lift me up in my new understanding of myself in all the ways that are healthy and harmonious for me.

This is a monumental change in my understanding of myself and my life. By coming to you and bringing you this, I ask for your support in living as [insert name/gender] in all the ways that are healthiest and most harmonious for me. I ask that you support me in my mind, my body, my spirit, my heart, my community, and the world around me. Making this change is not easy; I need allies among my gods and Ancestors and the land itself.

May the way always be open to me to make whatever changes I need to embody this truth about myself. May those I share this truth with hear it and acknowledge it and come to understand it. May I be protected from those who would deny or attack my sense of self and my newfound gender. May I find new friends, allies, and family to support me even further in this journey, living humans and spirits who can walk this path with me and guide me and aid me on it. May I be loved and appreciated and

known for who I truly am by all who look on me
and speak to me.

(You may wish to include more personalized things—asking for help with individual steps and parts of medical or social transition, really, any other requests for aid in regard to this that you need).

After you have said this, sit in the quiet for a few minutes. Listen and feel. Repeat the announcement if you feel unsure that it has been heard; repeat the requests if any of them weigh heavily on your heart or are a source of concern or anxiety. Pour your heart out to the Ancestors, gods, and land; they can hear you, and they can and will help you.

Speak to what you want in the future. Daydream out loud. Speak of the hopes and dreams you have for your new life; be as specific as possible and also as broad as you feel inclined to. This is an initiation, a new beginning; pray for what you would like to happen in this new life going forward.

If you use any particular kind of divination, now might be a good time to ask for omens or what kind of support you may be receiving. Understand this: The gods support you, and your Ancestors collectively will support you, even if not all of them individually agree. The Trans Dead will support you. You are not alone. Asking for your own health and wholeness is not going to make them angry (a lot of people worry about that). Nothing that you ask for is frivolous, foolish, or pointless; you deserve to have the support of the whole universe in all of your dreams and hopes going forward in your new understanding of yourself.

Once all that is done, spend a little bit more quiet time meditating or just listening. Listen to yourself and the world around you; listen to your gods and spirits if that is something you know how to do. Pay attention to anything that happens during this quiet period: the calls of birds or behavior of other animals, the wind and water and other elements, the light and how it rises or dims. There are voices and signs in all of these things; the powers speak to you with the voices of the world itself.

When you feel good and done, thank them—everyone who you have called out to so far. Put out the candle and incense, and walk forward into your new life knowing that you are whole and holy, loved and supported by the spiritual powers that guide your life. You may have some new allies as well.

Also, while I refer to this as a self-initiation, there's nothing saying that a friend who you know is supportive or a spiritual specialist or clergy that you respect can't be there and assist you in it as well. That also adds a bit of the social aspect of having a living human being present and witnessing, though the next ritual I include will focus more on that.

Community Gender Initiation

As we discussed above, sometimes an initiation takes place in a community context, and when it does, it almost always accompanies a change of social status, reflecting a new understanding of oneself and the recognition of that change among community. In many ways that's more of the norm: while spirit- and self-initiations are not uncommon, social initiations happen in a great many contexts: fraternities and sororities, prominent religious groups (baptism and confirmation are well-known Christian examples), joining societies and orders, and more.

Changing the way you present your gender is a massive life change and one that is often either acknowledged or rejected on a case-by-case basis by people. While on a deeply personal level that will always be true, community acknowledgment can be helpful because it is often self-reinforcing. Say someone comes out as transgender and a party is thrown where community members gather and acknowledge it publicly: the people who were there then have a responsibility to uphold and affirm the person's identity. If you've sat in witness (especially before the gods and Ancestors, for those who are religious) of the changes that a person has gone through, and welcomed and helped to affirm them, it becomes a responsibility to reaffirm these things when they are challenged or questioned. This can be especially helpful in individual communities such as in a religious group or coven, among family members, among classmates at school, or in other groups that someone might belong to. There's no need to stop at one or to tailor them to a one-size-fits-all event, either: different groups are going to have different values and ways that they express them, and ideally such a ceremony would be in alignment with the shared values of the group in such a way that it is meaningful to the individual members.

The popularity of gender reveal parties (often with disastrous environmental effects) has been on the rise, in no small way as a reaction to increased dialogue about transgender and nonbinary identity. While bragging about your infant's genitals is seen as uncouth in most settings, somehow doing so in this particular setting is considered acceptable. Along with your infant's genitals, people who perform gender reveal parties are declaring their expectations about their child's preferences and path in life: they will like these colors, they will hold this reproductive role, they will be interested in these things. If you've read this far, I don't have to go overboard explaining how harmful that can be to *any* child. Setting up these expectations about how a child will grow and develop is cruel because inevitably when they do not meet those expectations there is regret on the part of the parents and social circle. Infants are too young to tell people what their gender is, much less their career path and reproductive goals; gender reveal parties amount to nonconsensual social initiations for the infant, emphasizing that based on their genitals they are part of a particular social grouping that they have no way of agreeing to.

The idea of reclaiming gender reveals for transgender and nonbinary people has grown in popularity over the years, although to some extent we have always had those. What a wonderful idea to have a party where a community acknowledges the gender of the individual and members of that gender (should any be present) provide them with things that are socially useful to folks of that gender: advice, promises of support, and shared acts of fellowship. This provides the affirmation from the community of identity and change of status and the implicit support and acknowledgment of the person as they understand themselves to be.

The framework used above for the gender self-initiation could be used on a larger community scale. The ritual could be performed and administered with the help of members of the community who are close to the transgender or nonbinary individual, with the clergy or helpers assisting them in reciting lines and doing a call-and-response with the subject of the rite.

It would also be possible to include a shared oath, something to the effect of,

> We have all witnessed this declaration, and we promise to support [person's name] in their identity. We will correct one another and strangers if they are misgendered or deadnamed; we will provide social support in navigating life as a [person's gender]. Among us they will not only be accepted or tolerated but fully celebrated for who they are. May the gods and Ancestors aid and support us all in this.

Shared oaths like this have powerful social and metaphysical effects on those who take them and those who witness them; the guiding powers of the people involved take note and most likely will provide guidance and strength to those who are complying with it.

Such a ceremony doesn't need to be entirely magical or spiritual, however. The spiritual portion of it could be a single part of a larger event or could be spread out bit by bit through the event. Other things that might be valuable could include:

- New clothing that matches the person's style and understanding of their gender

- Gift cards for places where the person can receive gender-affirming items, treatments, or clothing

- Games that are associated with that person's understanding of their gender

- Advice or stories about shared gendered experiences (Be careful with advice, though; the purpose is to make the subject of the ritual feel included, not berated, and as always, make sure that advice is welcome before dispensing it.)
- Invitations to events that this person associates with their newly acknowledged gender

There are many more potential gifts or events that could be part of this kind of ceremony. The most important part is that the person is publicly acknowledged by their shared community, listened to when they explain their experience of and understanding of their gender, and hears the affirmation that those present will support them in the ways that they ask for around this difficult transition in their lives.

Gender can be very individual and idiosyncratic, as we've pointed out; understandings of it vary not just culture-to-culture but person-to-person within that culture. Grace and validation should be provided to the subject's own understanding of their gender; far too often, trans and nonbinary people are told "what it means to be a woman/a man/nonbinary" by people with very specific ideas about these things that may not mesh well with their understanding. This is about supporting your community member and letting them and the rest of the community know that you support them, not imposing your idea of how someone of their gender should live. I will provide the same advice in this that I always do when folks ask how to treat a trans person: ask them, listen to them, give them opportunities to express the things that they are feeling. They know who and what they are better than anyone else; respect that and listen, and you can't go wrong.

Rite of Becoming

On the one hand, we know that gender is an internal thing. As the saying among trans folks goes, "Wanting to be a girl is a symptom of being a girl." You are who you know yourself to be.

On the other hand, we know that society treats us a particular way based off of our appearance and mannerisms. We may know the truth locked inside of us, but that bringing it forward is another story. It is a difficult work, and for many trans folks, a central work in becoming oneself.

Social and medical transition can be difficult to obtain or attain. For a great many of us, while we know ourselves to be who we are inside, bringing that out in a way that is reflected in the world around us is difficult.

Change requires compromise. It requires sacrifice. Sacrifice is difficult and painful, even when the results are joyous. It can be hard to do that when you aren't sure of the trade-off. This is one of the things that makes huge changes in your life, like losing weight or finishing a school program, difficult: you don't have something to hang on to as a reminder of what you're trying to achieve. It's also possible for your goals to shift over time; what you want, as well as your understanding of yourself, can change.

Here is a simple rite and spell to help you keep these things in alignment. The principles behind it are simple, and the practice of it is simple as well. It combines spirit and deity work, affirmations, and good old-fashioned spellcraft.

First, begin by going over some of the things that you have isolated and pulled forward going through the Elements of Gender chapter. Gather together the pieces of your identity and sense of self that you want to bring forward into your body and life. Take each one and consider it: how would this look if applied to me in the way that I want it to be? What would this look like when it developed from a seed in my consciousness into a full-blown aspect of myself, something that is not only internal but also something that people associate with me? Write a little bit about it, a sentence at most for each one.

Once you have done that, take a look at what you have written for each element of your gender. Try reading them out loud. Is there a way that you can arrange those descriptions into a poem or song? Can you find a rhythm you like? You can put as much work into this as you want to, or as little; the goal is to have a repeatable chant or invocation or song that you will be using for this. If all you can manage is a grocery list of your elements with a couple of words after each, then that's what you can manage, and it will likely work for you. However, embellishing it helps to formalize it in your mind; the work you do on it will attract the attention of your gods and spirits, and making a whole invocation that you feel proud of will definitely help fuel your success and magic.

A bit of inspiration that might be helpful: I've heard many transmasculine friends express love for the lyrics of "I'll Make a Man Out of You" from Disney's *Mulan*. Even if you aren't trying to embody that particular gender, it is a wonderful example of a poem containing the elements the character singing it considers to be essential to manhood. It and other songs like that may serve as a good pattern for the kind of poem, prayer, or spell you are trying to write.

Now that you have that written, consider again sacred connections between these elements and powers that you respect and honor. We go a little bit into this in the Elements of Gender chapter, but here I want you to give some thought to who you will be calling on for help in bringing these elements forward in your life. Mark each element with the name of the power that you are calling on: they can all be the same being or many different ones. Incorporate them each into their respective elements; it can look like "Hail and praise to so-and-so who embodies this quality; please bless me with it and help me to develop it," or even just have their name spoken at the beginning and end of each element, as in, "[Deity], quality, [Deity]."

This might take a little bit of time to work on; not everyone has experience in working with this sort of thing. If you feel stuck on powers associated with the elements that you are including, look through the chapter Gods and Gender; there are a few examples there, and I speak from personal experience that at very least Dionysos, Ariadne, and Kybele are all willing to support this kind of work. Don't worry about making it perfect, and don't worry about including everything; this is a work in progress, just as we are all works in progress. Once you have all the elements you've thought of expressed in this invocation, set it aside.

Consider the powers you are calling on for this work. Do you already have relationships with them? Consider if any of the powers that you already work with have intersections with what you are trying to achieve. If not, before petitioning them, at very least make an offering to them and ask them for help and guidance in this work; while it's possible to call a stranger who is known for helping folks like you without any kind of background, an introduction and a shared gift is always a good way to start a relationship. Make sure that you do this at least once for every being you are calling to.

Now you have a full invocation and have made a basic connection with each being involved with that invocation. Write out the invocation on a piece of paper that you can read it from; spend some time and attention making it look nice. Feel free to draw symbols, runes, and images on it that embody the elements you are looking to incorporate, as well as sacred symbols for the powers you are calling on for this work. This piece of paper will be like a sacred scroll for you and a part of the spell. Make it as pleasing to you as you can in whatever way works, with pleasing colors of paper and ink, possibly applying oil or perfume that you feel strongly about or that is connected to the powers being invoked, or by adding glitter or other decorations. Sprinkle it with sacred ash from incense burned for the powers being invoked in this rite. If you have a connection between your gender and its elements and a deity associated with a heavenly body like the sun, the moon, or a planet, leave the paper out while that heavenly body is in the sky to soak up some of the energies from it. When you are not working on it, keep it in a safe place, preferably whatever altar or shrine space you have set up. While you want this paper to be well-embellished and empowered, also remember not to let the perfect be the enemy of the good; this can be done more than once, so don't worry about getting every little thing perfect. Set a date for yourself to be done by (preferably a new moon) and work with what you have by then.

Finally, draw a labyrinth at the top of the paper. (You can find instructions for drawing a simple labyrinth online pretty easily.)

Once this is done, take your magical scroll and pick a good date for it. I recommend the new moon as a time of beginnings. If you're into astrology, you can try and chart for a specific configuration or beneficial aspect; it can't hurt.

Prepare yourself as you would for any rite. Do some basic cleansing and space-setting and creation of boundaries. Greet and make offerings to the land, the Ancestors, and the gods as general categories.

Once you have done that, go ahead and perform whatever invocations you like to the beings called to in your spell. Greet them and welcome them to the space. Make some kind of offerings to them specifically as well.

Once everyone has been called, issue a statement of purpose. It could be something like,

> *Blessed powers, I have called you here today to assist me in this working. I need assistance in bringing forth my true self, helping to bring together these elements of my identity into manifestation in my life. Help me to embody these qualities; help me to change myself and the world around me in the ways that are necessary for them to come to fruition and be manifest. I ask for you to assist me in whatever way you can with this, in harmony with one another and my highest good.*

Take your sacred scroll of manifestation and read from it. Even if you already know your spell by heart, read it from the scroll, reciting it over and over. You can do this a magically significant number of times based on your traditions and personal practice, but three, seven, and nine are always popular (though five is also an option given its association with change in Pythagorean numerology). You can also take an ecstatic approach to it; read it in a singsong voice or as a chant, starting with your voice lower and building up speed and power until you feel it reach a peak. The repetition is important: it cements it in your mind, it firmly establishes to the powers being invoked what your request is, and it raises energy that then will be directed toward this end. You may also anoint the scroll at this point with drops of liquid or ash from offerings.

Once this is done, thank the powers, take down the space, end the rite, and tuck the paper away somewhere safe. You can roll it up and tie it off with yarn or a cord, tuck it into a sacred book, or put it underneath an image of a power involved in this work or even under your altar cloth. Just make sure that you keep it somewhere in your sacred space so that it is constantly interacting with the energies of your powers and kept away from mundane things.

The paper can be brought out and carried like a talisman if you are going to do things that will help bring about the qualities you are looking for. Are you going for a surgery consultation? Hair removal? A class for a particular craft, sport, or practice that you associate with one of your elements? Having a difficult conversation about your identity? Take the paper, fold it in any way that makes sense and won't damage it, and carry it in a special pouch or container with you while you do these things. Having a rough dysphoria day? Keep it on you as a reminder that you are working toward a time when that dysphoria will no longer be present, and as a reminder that you are a work in progress yourself. While you aren't yet where you want to be, someday you will be. When you prepare to take it with you, recite the spell on it, and do the same when you go to put it away. Treat it as the sacred object that it is, and make sure it always finds its way home to the shrine, altar, or other sacred space that you keep it in.

What happens when your goals change or when your sense of self shifts? In this case, I suggest creating a new one using the old one as a guide. You can repeat the new moon ritual for it, and before enchanting the new paper, take the old one, thank the powers for their assistance in it, and explain that your goals and direction have changed. Dispose of it in whatever way feels right; burning is always magically significant and has connotations of rebirth, transformation, and the phoenix, and burying is often connected to returning things to their roots and the world.

Gender Sigils

When we speak of sigil creation in modern magic, we are often speaking of a popular magical practice that has its roots in chaos magic and the work of Austin Osman Spare (though it certainly has grown quite a bit since then). Chaos magic is not about chaos but about finding the most basic elements required for magic to work, applied with a framework chosen or created arbitrarily by the magician.

Regardless, the standard popular method of sigil creation runs something like this:

1. Find a statement about a thing you desire to come about. Phrase it as a thing that has already happened.

2. Write it down. Remove all the vowels and all of the duplicate letters.

3. Take the remaining letters and arrange them into a single symbol that is pleasing to your aesthetic or spiritual paradigm.

4. Activate the sigil. People often recommend staring at the sigil during orgasm or some other experience that takes one outside themselves.

5. Destroy the sigil and do your best to forget about it.

Each of the stages has a reason or justification for it, but it has never really worked for me, and I'm not alone in that. Other proponents of sigil magic suggest more fluid takes: simply using meaningful symbols to construct a simple meta-symbol and do whatever kind of magic you do to activate the sigil.

I've come up with my own method of sigil work based on animist and polytheist practice, and I'll share that here in conjunction with ideas related to sigils to help you affect the gender expression that you want to or do other gender-related things.

In my own animist understanding, sigils and most forms of magic work because spirits of the things involved, or the spirit of the Universe itself, agree to make it happen and work toward that goal. This is a cocreation with the magician and can be accomplished in many ways, but at its most basic, animist magic involves negotiating with the animating personalities of reality.

To do this kind of sigil magic in this framework, it helps to have beings and spirits to call to. Fortunately, you do; most spiritual practices suggest that we have Ancestors, personal spirits, guardian angels, daimons, or other entities that work with and for us specifically. These beings who stand close to you are there to interface with greater beings or those further removed; they act as messengers, translators, and enactors of your will or the will of those who assigned them to you in the first place, or a combination thereof. Many people in modern practice will casually refer to their "team," one's "team" being the collective of beings of all varieties and levels who are there for you. Your "team" in this context is generally considered beings who are smaller or less potent than deities, ones that are more personal, and specifically ones that are related to you.

Getting to know your team is a great work for any spiritual practitioner and not one that I can go into in detail here; it deserves more space, time, and context. Simply knowing that you have allies who are there for your highest good and calling to them, especially along with calling the blessings of your gods, is usually enough to get their attention and a worthwhile practice in and of itself.

Here are the steps:

1. Identify what you want to embody.

    What changes do you want to make? Is this about how you see yourself, how other people see you (and which ones), how spirits or gods see you? If you are trying to embody something that you don't feel is manifest in some way, your motivations are important, and in this case the source of your motivations is your audience. Do you need to calm the inner pain you have about a body feature? Then this is for you. Is this so people are more likely to gender you correctly? Then it's for them. Think about the effect that you want to achieve, whether it involves changing your body, your behavior, or other people's perception of you.

The potential applications of this magic for trans and nonbinary people (and for cisgender folks who are interested in experimenting with their gender) are nearly limitless. Magic needs to be carefully targeted, however, and the easiest path to the actual goal is often the most likely to succeed. "People read my voice as X" is easier than "My voice is indistinguishable from a cis person of X gender." Because in many cases changing your actual voice is more difficult than nudging things in the right direction to ensure you are read the way that you want to be read. Consider what the easiest way to accomplish that goal would be. Consider the way major goals are made up of smaller goals; it's often easier with this sort of magic to target individual smaller portions of a larger outcome than it is to pull a major change all at once.

2. Find symbols that correlate to the elements of what you want to embody.

Next, you're going to develop a set of symbols to make into a "sentence." Don't worry too much about things like grammar or syntax; you can go full cave-enby on this if you want. "Everyone hear me as [woman/

man]," "HRT make boobs big," "Testosterone go BRR-RRR"—it doesn't need to be elegant or eloquent because the language that you're translating these concepts into isn't the language you speak with your mouth but the one that you speak with your spirit.

For each component of your "sentence," find or make a symbol. It can be something as simple as an arrow or complex as a graph. Simpler can be better because you're going to want to play with the symbol a bit, but if you like making complicated sigils and the challenge of it is part of the experience for you, go for it! They can be quite beautiful. If you have figured out some things you consider elements of your gender from the Elements of Gender chapter, you could work them all together to create a gender sigil, something to wear or keep on you to resonate with those energies and concepts.

Some easy symbol ideas to play with: T, P, E for testosterone, progesterone, estrogen, Venus symbol for women/feminine, Mars symbol for men/masculine, Mercury symbol for nonbinary (or any other planetary symbol for nonbinary! Nonbinary isn't a single thing! And neither is man or woman), eyes for being seen, ears for being heard.

If the symbol is something that's very standard, put a small twist on it to make it unique—a curl or a flair. I don't recommend this with runes, but that's my personal preference. If you are skilled with runes and do that all the time, then I'm not going to try and stop you; magic is about what works.

3. Arrange those symbols in a meaningful way.

The next step is to create a whole picture with these symbols. A good way to do that is to align parts of them with one another so that their lines overlap, but not completely. Even if you're just using letters, there are a lot of ways that can look, so feel free to play with them. I find that making sigils appear evocative of their subject is helpful; if it's something to help a dog heal, I will try and shape it like a happy dog. I also recognize that there's only so much you can do sometimes, but it can be a very helpful technique and will aid you and the spirits in correctly recognizing the meaning of the sigil.

Other ways to arrange the symbols is to draw them all inside a circle or other sacred shape, or to string them along a line like a strip of dangling decorations. As long as they are connected, that's what matters.

4. Call on your gods and your team to recognize those symbols individually and the meaning of the combined symbol.

Now for the ritual portion of things: do the ritual prep that you do—cleansing, setting of space, etc. Consider which gods and spirits you want to assist you in this work. Call to them, provide them with good offerings, and ask them to take up your case. Once you have called them, explain aloud what those symbols mean to you and how you would like the gods and entities to act on them. Put your passion and desire into the request, pouring your heart into it; let them know what you need and why. If you have any divination tools, go ahead and divine on the result; some adjustments may be required and guidance will be provided if that is the case.

5. Put that symbol into use.

Once you have created a symbol and gotten the support of your powers in the use of it, it can be used in a lot of different ways:

+ Draw the symbol on a piece of paper; burn it in offering to the beings who have empowered it. Do this any time you need an extra-powerful boost.

+ If you wear a fragrance or use any kind of holy water, you can draw the symbol with it on your skin, on your clothes, or over pictures and images of you (such as the ID that you carry)—anything that represents you.

+ You can scribble it into the margins of things that you are writing, draw it on your skin with skin-safe marker or eyeliner pen, sketch it with a phone app and put it up as a phone background (or add it to an existing image for your phone background).

+ Draw it on the ground and pour offerings over it near somewhere that you walk regularly.

+ Wood burn it, sketch it, engrave it on a bead to work into a piece of jewelry or just as a charm you carry with you in your pocket.

There are a lot of ways to incorporate your sigils. The only warning I have is not to make them permanent, i.e., as a tattoo or some kind of permanent marking on your body. What you want or your understanding of yourself may shift over time, and you don't want to be locked in to any one particular image or understanding of yourself.

I'm going to note that while this is the order I suggest you do these things in, you can absolutely switch things up. Animism and polytheism are relational, and magic in these contexts is co-creative. If the people you trust are telling you to switch things up from what I have here, please consider their wisdom.

In addition, if you are using symbols that are from traditions where they have specific magical uses, try to use them in alignment with their original purpose, or your magic will not be as effective and may actually backfire. You almost certainly do not want to use the Thurisaz rune to represent your desire to rock a girl bulge; there are plenty of phallic runes that have more appropriate connotations. Again, this is cocreation, and some of this has already been created. It is difficult to reassign meaning to ancient and well-established symbols; not all of the spirits (including the spirits of the symbols themselves) are likely to be on board with uses that are radically different from their common use. At the same time, those same spirits may have good suggestions for alternate symbols or a different framing for the symbol that puts it into alignment with what you want.

Prayer of Protection

As we've said before, being transgender or nonbinary isn't safe. We don't get much of a choice in that; for as tight as our communities may be, there are always times when we need to venture into the cisgender world. It can be scary being brave, alone, out there, and you in a human society that doesn't want you. I know this from personal experiences.

I'm providing this prayer for protection here. I know Kybele will respond to the call of a trans person for protection, and I know that our Ancestors will listen to us and give us support. Obviously you may have your own deities and spirits to call on in addition, and I encourage you to add to this prayer if you want to incorporate them.

Prayers for protection don't do well by being long-winded; when you're asking for safety, you don't usually have the luxury of making lengthy petitions. Also, don't worry so much about offerings if you're praying for safety; show your appreciation once you're out of danger.

Say,

> *Kybele protect me,*
> *Send me your lions.*
> *Trans Ancestors protect me,*
> *Send me your strength.*
> *Stand between me and harm.*
> *Keep me safe and whole and healthy.*
> *Blessings and thanks.*

And that's it; that's all you need to get their attention and call on them for help. I pray that you never need to, but don't forget: you are not alone, and you have spiritual allies as well as mundane ones to stand by your side.

GLOSSARY

agender: Someone who does not have a gender or who has no felt sense of connection to any gender.

bigender: Someone with two genders, sometimes fluid between them and sometimes simultaneously.

birth assignment: The gender that someone was assigned at birth, usually by medical professionals and parents. Shortened to AGAB (assigned gender at birth).

cisgender: Someone who identifies as the gender they were assigned at birth. For example, if the doctor decided that someone was a girl and they are a girl, they are cisgender.

cissexism: The assumption that being cisgender is the default, along with the forms of oppression that occur based on that assumption.

demiboy/girl: A demiboy or demigirl is someone who feels partly but not wholly associated with boy or girl.

enby: A short way of saying "nonbinary" from "(n)on (b)inary." Generally refers to a person. "I'm an enby" rather than "I'm enby."

gender binary: The idea that there are only two genders, man and woman, and that they are immutable and based on biology.

genderfluid: Someone whose gender shifts. It may shift between the two popular genders or between different nonbinary genders; genderfluid just means that one's sense of gender (and often, but not always, gender presentation) shifts.

gender identity: One's own sense of gender; what one knows oneself to be.

gender presentation: The outward trappings of appearance and behavior associated with a gender. The gender that a person presents as socially.

misogyny: Prejudice against women, sometimes applied to people perceived to be women who are not.

neopronouns: Pronouns that aren't in common English usage; any pronouns sets that aren't she/her, he/him, or they/them. Popular examples include: sie/hir, zie/zir, fae/faer, e/em/es, though there are a great many possibilities.

nonbinary: Gender that lies outside of the standard division of male and female. Nonbinary isn't a single thing; there are many nonbinary genders, and being agender is considered nonbinary by many. Also used as a noun for a person who is nonbinary.

nonbinary man or woman: A person whose understanding of themselves contains *man* or *woman* but also has a nonbinary element.

pronouns: A word that can function the same as a noun in referring to someone or something in speech and writing. Common pronouns are he/him, she/her, they/them, and it/its. While *he* and *she* are primarily associated with masculine and feminine gender, a person may use any pronoun for themselves regardless of gender.

sexism: Discrimination or prejudice on the basis of sex or gender.

transfeminine: A modifier describing a person who was assigned male at birth but who takes on characteristics that are considered to be feminine. Most trans women are transfeminine; not all transfeminine people are women (many are nonbinary).

transgender: An umbrella term for people whose gender identity does not match the gender that they were assigned at birth.

transition: The general term for the process of changing one's gender presentation and expression to match one's actual gender rather than the gender assigned at birth. Includes social transition (changing social role, name, pronouns, etc.) and medical transition (hormone therapy, surgical intervention, other medical assistance in transition). Transition is not necessary for someone to be transgender; a transgender person is someone whose birth assignment does not correspond to their actual gender.

trans man: A transgender man, i.e., a man who was assigned female at birth.

transmasculine: A modifier describing a person who was assigned female at birth but who takes on characteristics that are considered to be masculine. Most trans men are transmasculine; not all transmasculine people are men (many are nonbinary).

transmisogyny: Prejudice against transgender women and transfeminine people.

trans woman: A transgender woman, i.e., a woman who was assigned male at birth.

xenogender: Someone whose experience of gender aligns with something that isn't human, e.g., a star, a forest, a color, a faun.

BIBLIOGRAPHY

Aristides, Aelius. *Orations.* Edited and translated by Michael Trapp. 2 vols. Loeb Classical Library. Cambridge, MA: Harvard University Press, 2017.

Athanassakis, Apostolos N., and Benjamin M. Wolkow, trans., *The Orphic Hymns.* Baltimore, MD: John Hopkins University Press, 2013.

Carter, Mark. *Stalking the Goddess.* Alresford, UK: Moon Books, 2012.

Graf, Fritz, and Sarah Iles Johnston. *Ritual Texts for the Afterlife: Orpheus and the Bacchic Gold Tablets.* New York: Routledge, 2007.

Grammaticus, Saxo. *The First Nine Books of the Danish History of Saxo Grammaticus.* Translated by Oliver Elton. With additional material by Frederick York Powell. London: D. Nutt, 1894.

Johnston, Sarah Iles. *Hekate Soteira: A Study of Hekate's Role in the Chaldean Oracles and Related Literature.* Atlanta, GA: Scholar Press, 1990.

Lokasenna. In *The Poetic Edda: Translated from the Icelandic with an Introduction and Notes.* Scandinavian Classics Volumes XXI and XXII. Translated by Henry Adams Bellows. New York: The American Scandinavian Foundation, 1923.

Lewis, Clive Staples. *Till We Have Faces.* Orlando, FL: Harcourt & Brace, 1980.